FROM THE EMPIRE STATE TO THE VAMPIRE STATE

New York In A Downward Transition

Herbert London
and
Edwin S. Rubenstein

UNIVERSITY
PRESS OF
AMERICA

Lanham • New York • London

Copyright © 1994 by
University Press of America,® Inc.
4720 Boston Way
Lanham, Maryland 20706

3 Henrietta Street
London WC2E 8LU England

Library of Congress Cataloging-in-Publication Data
London, Herbert Ira.
From the Empire State to the vampire state : New York in a
downward transition / Herbert London and Edwin S. Rubenstein.
p.   cm.
1. Political planning—New York (State)   2. New York (State,—
Politics and government—1951–   3. New York (State)—Economic
policy.   4. New York (State)—Social policy.   5. Politicians—New
York (State)—Interviews.   I. Rubinstein, Edwin S.   II. Title.
JK3438   1994   320.9747'09'048—dc20   94–20687 CIP

ISBN 0–8191–9605–3 (pbk. : alk. paper)

The paper used in this publication meets the minimum requirements of
American National Standard for Information Sciences—Permanence
of Paper for Printed Library Materials, ANSI Z39.48–1984.

To thoughtful and understanding wives

Contents

Preface

This book is both an analytical and political document. It plumbs the depths of statistical analysis and refines judgments through interviews with an assemblage of bipartisan observers of the New York political and economic landscape.

Several people played an important role in this project and should be acknowledged. Those interviewed contributed their forthright opinions with patience and generosity. Dorit Moskovich assembled the pieces, typed them and deciphered the sometimes impenetrable prose. Carol Kahn Strauss contributed her abundant editorial skill. For these efforts we are grateful.

Although some will contend this book is a partisan review, we can assure those doubters that every effort was made to be fair. If New York appears as a state in despair, that judgment is supported by the evidence. New York is no longer the state it once was; it is as our hope that this book will serve as a catalyst for the long overdue recovery.

H.L.
E.R.

Introduction

A recent study by Grant Thornton, a Chicago based survey firm, indicates that North Carolina ranks number one as having the best "manufacturing climate" among 29 industrial states. The state's relatively modest wages, low unemployment, and low taxes contribute to its hospitable environment for business. In contrast, New York ranked number 23.

New York's negative rating results from a combination of its high average hourly wages, high percentage of union workers, high employment and workers' compensation benefits, high state taxes, and poor education systems. The level of employee education has become a special concern, according to this annual survey. The report notes that "Manufacturers are feeling the pinch of educational systems that produce workers who can neither read, write nor perform simple arithmetic. Teaching their employees such basic skills is a substantial expense."

Education was only second to wages in the concerns measured by the 1993 survey. The year before, it was the eighth most important issue in a review of 16 factors. Following wages and education, the most pressing issues are workers' overall compensation (benefits) and unionization.

While not definitive, these kinds of ratings do create impressions that cannot be underestimated. At some point other kinds of market conditions, such as relatively low rents for office space, may alter the perception of whether a state is a good place to do business, but in the short term, the fundamental factors are what count.

It is astonishing that New York's public servants don't appear to have the foggiest idea of what constitutes a congenial business environment. Among policymakers, taxes and a depreciation of educational quality seem to be unrelated to business decisions. These officials assume a static economic climate, independent of all the factors that effect it. The fact that 2.1 million New Yorkers have left the state in the last 14 years should demonstrate beyond a shadow of doubt that for most of these people, there is something wrong with the state's economy. For Albany, such departures are little more than business as usual.

Clearly, perceptions die hard. Even if New York's governor and legislature were to lower taxes, it would take some time before business leaders perceived a real change. Moreover, there are many other considerations for a business location, including rail and highway transportation, water supply, proximity to raw materials and availability of markets. Unfortunately, here, too, New York comes up short.

The state's highway system is in desperate need of repair. While water, particularly fresh water, is one of the state's greatest assets, it is a resource under constant pressure from various lobbying groups. Rigid, sometimes obtuse and counterproductive environmental laws, seem to endorse an unrealistically pristine environment instead of economic development. Markets are shifting, especially to the south and west. But when New Yorkers leave the state, they don't necessarily depart for the greener pastures of Florida, Arizona and California. Instead they move to New Jersey, Connecticut and Pennsylvania.

According to the governor's 1993 executive budget, taxes and fees will increase by $1.9 billion. Of this sum, $730 million represents the cancellation of the last stage of the personal income tax cut passed in 1987. This tax hike comes on the heels of billion-dollar-plus tax and fee increases in 1989, 1990, 1991, and 1992. In fact, total spending (the entire budget including the often overlooked off-budget expenditures) will increase by $3.2 billion.

Approximately $670 million in one-shot fiscal arrangements is proposed in the new budget, on top of the more than $7 billion in one-shots adopted in New York since 1985. These include the repurchase of Attica prison, the Erie Canal system, the Aqueduct Race Track parking lot, and the New York State Thruway, to cite several of the many egregious examples. In addition, the governor is proposing to issue $531 million in "deficit notes" to offset the anticipated budget gap, a gap that will rise to over $3 billion in 1995.

As part of his 1992 State of the State address, the governor said that due to the anemic economy recovery, a tonic in the form of $800 million in public works programs would be attached to his budget proposal. If ever there was an idea discredited by the march of events, it is this one. But apparently the governor is trying to adopt something, anything, that will give the appearance of a silver lining. By 1994, in his State of the State address, the governor was trying to transform himself into a born-again supply-sider with his claim that only lower taxes can promote private sector jobs.

On the welfare and Medicaid front - which accounts for 41 percent of the state budget - the governor's reforms have much thunder and little lightening. There are new provider-side taxes and assessments, as well as reimbursement adjustments, for an increase of $743 million, while programmatic reform accounts for $87 million. His approach can easily be contrasted with former Governor Jim Florio, a Democrat on the western side of the Hudson, who has introduced bold reforms in New Jersey such as workfare and restricted eligibility for assistance.

Although Governor Cuomo has described his budget as "lean" and filled with "significant reforms," it is, in our opinion, a budget that is overweight, overly reliant on new taxes, and without the imagination found in Wisconsin and California budgets. It is replete with more of the same schemes we have encountered in New York over the last decade. Through financial *legerdemain*, the governor will attempt to convince the legislative leaders that his budget is in the best interest of the state. But his argument, no matter how artfully delivered, won't wash.

New York is not in the economic doldrums because of insufficient assistance from the federal government. Federal sharing to New York State has gone up from $12 billion in 1990 to $17.8 in 1992. Of course, whatever Washington gives will be spent: the measure of appropriate federal spending for the New York State government is whatever it will take to cover the budget deficit. So while more funding from Washington would make Governor Cuomo happy, it's not likely to be forthcoming.

George Will, the noted political analyst, columnist and author (including a current bestselling book on baseball) contends that the referendum on Proposition III in California, which could ease the spending limits imposed on the state in 1979 under the so-called Gann limit, is the litmus test for reform of state spending practices. He argues that there is a pent-up need for state spending. While Will is most certainly correct in asserting that what happens in California is likely to affect the rest of us, he avoids the central question of the wisdom of expanding the state's spending authority.

The so-called Gann limit is primarily why California bonds are in demand and highly rated, while New York bonds are zooming southward as recent bond ratings attest. In the almost twelve years under Governor Mario Cuomo, state spending has increased 130 percent, close to three times the rate of inflation and about twice the rate of California.

What Will ignores is that it is easy to develop a legislative consensus for spending and hard to organize bipartisan support for cuts. Moreover, government spending rarely takes into account those state responsibilities that are essential and separates them from those that are peripheral. Nor is state spending evaluated against a backdrop in which the borrowing capacity of private entrepreneurs is crowded out of financial markets by state borrowers.

State governments do indeed have an obligation to perform certain services, such as the maintenance of public order and upkeep of the infrastructure. But the excessive accumulation of state authority at the expense of the taxpayer is, in most instances, not warranted. If the states were to put a premium on privatizing services, significant savings could occur.

In New York State, for example, the government played a prominent role in privatizing the port of Buffalo, saving the taxpayers millions of dollars; yet the same principle has not been applied to the privatization of the Albany or Stewart airports. By enrolling New York Medicaid recipients in the privately operated Empire State Medical Health Plan, the state could save over $700 million. This is not inconsiderable, especially since the state's Medicaid system is the fastest-growing item in the New York budget. In addition, the Empire plan is so comprehensive that a majority of state employees opt for its coverage rather than a state provided plan which is offered free of charge.

These recommendations are merely the tip of the proverbial iceberg. By selling the state's passenger car fleet and contracting with rental companies, New York could save at least $3.7 million annually. By transferring civil service testing to a private firm, it could save $4 million. By contracting prison health services to private local providers, the state could save $12 million.

One might ask why, when between 1984 and 1989 the State University of New York had an enrollment decline of nearly 6,000 students, the size of the SUNY staff increased by 4,300 and spending increased 60 percent from $2 billion to $3.2 billion. Or why the state operates ski sites which could be leased to private operators, thereby increasing revenue and reducing costs. Similarly, one might want to know why the state provides a major subvention to a cheese museum. (If this museum offers aesthetic attributes unavailable in other museums, perhaps its patrons should pay for the privilege of their edification.) If contract maintenance services were more widely used in government offices, the state could save about 25 percent from its maintenance budget.   In fact, if the state counterpart to a N.Y. City Grace Commission were established, not only could spending be controlled, it could be rolled back.

The Will hypothesis that there is a pent-up need for state spending is misleading. There may be a need for spending in some areas, but there is assuredly gross overspending in others. In order to create an economic climate congenial to business activity and productive labor, the state has an obligation to cut spending so that it can cut taxes.

When Governor Cuomo reneged on his promised tax cut, he sent a message to New Yorkers that will most assuredly result in a shrinking state tax base. The Gann spending limit in California may seem arbitrary, but it is not as capricious as the ten percent plus annual budgetary increases in New York. If Will wants to see California bond ratings plummet as was the case in New York, all one has to do lift the ban that prohibits legislators from excess spending.

New York is not merely a state, it is (or was) a state of mind. For midwesterners, New York's gravitational pull was irresistible. This was the center of an electric field. To be in New York was to be infused with energy. However, like all energy fields, this one is losing its spark. New York has even lost its metaphorical clout: "if you can make it there, you can make it anywhere" doesn't have the same resonance it once did. In fact, the refrain is now sung by homeless people in a television commercial soliciting funds for charitable assistance.

While the state's economy has slowed down significantly since the mid-1980s, and while New York has lagged behind contiguous states, it still grew faster over the last decade than the national average. There are actually more than one million new New Yorkers paying taxes today than when Governor Mario Cuomo was first elected in 1982. Tax revenues have increased by 89 percent since 1983, while inflation has gone up by 45 percent in this same period.

Based on these facts, one might assume that all is well in the Empire State. However, from a fiscal standpoint conditions couldn't be much worse. New York has lost its luster, in large part because spending has increased at a rate well in excess of revenue retrieval. If there is a fiscal crisis, an assertion even Mr. Cuomo can't deny, it isn't due to the recessionary climate, or President Reagan and Bush's policies, or a revenue shortfall; it is due to dazzling spending increases.

Governor Cuomo and the state legislature appear determined to raise New Yorkers' taxes by over $1 billion for the fifth year in a row. The push for new taxes comes from politicians who seem unable to fathom a world in which New York chooses to cut the budget of government rather than the budgets of New York families.

In the Brave New World of Albany politicians, the governor has proposed a budget for 1994 that cuts spending by $4.5 billion. What is little understood is that this so-called cut is from a projection that holds if - and only if - spending is left unchecked in the new fiscal year. In other words, the cuts are in projected increases. In the real world, the governor's proposed budget will still increase spending by over $3 billion (instead of $7.5 billion).

If you ask an Albany politician why he doesn't cut spending further - possibly freeze it for one year - he will tell you the budget has already been cut to the bone. This is preposterous.

We have developed a plan to cut spending by $5 to $6 billion and avoid the need for one cent more in taxes. And no, we would not take food out of the mouths of babies or cut off aid to low-or-middle-income students or throw elderly people on the streets.

There are common-sense solutions that will cut waste, make government more responsive than it is, and eliminate indefensible subsidies for the rich.

If three items could be cut (education, Medicaid, and welfare) - without adversely affecting services delivered - taxes would not have to rise and spending need not increase to the tune of 5.9 percent, as Governor Cuomo has prescribed.

Starting with education, the aid formula should be correlated to a reduction of district administrative budgets. The state and local educational bureaucracy is far too large for services rendered. Similarly, the central administration of CUNY and SUNY should be consolidated. If a means test were introduced for tuition payment at public colleges and universities, offering an element of equity in the tuition schedule, and the actual tuition of $15,000 were used as a guide, the state would gain something on the order of $60 million in revenues.

If Medicaid reimbursement rates were indexed using 1990 as a benchmark year, significant savings would accrue to the state. A redistribution of fees to physicians and hospital clinics would also have a mitigating effect on the budget strain. Medicaid eligible children under age 18 can be transferred to the NY-Child Health care plan with dramatic cost savings. At least one half of the non-elderly in the Medicaid population can be transferred to HMO's or preferred provider organizations, thereby saving money and improving preventive care. At last, efforts should be made to cut expenditures and offer care facilities at levels comparable to the present service.

By any measure, the New York State welfare system is overly expensive and inefficient. The budget in the Department of Social Services is $160 million, and this department doesn't issue a single welfare check. If the Department of Social Services were eliminated with a new umbrella agency handling Medicaid, and if welfare concerns were organized in a manner consistent with federal government regulations, inefficiency and redundancy could be eliminated. If foster care assistance for relatives were placed at the low end of the graduated assistance budget, unless the specifics of a case deem otherwise, substantial savings for the state can be generated.

It is time to break the tax-spend-elect cycle in Albany. The choice for Governor Cuomo and state legislators is clear: they can side with the overburdened New York taxpayers or they can coddle up to the special interest lobbyists once again. Based on my (Herb London) campaign for governor in 1990, we can assure Albany's politicians that a grassroots tax revolt is brewing in this state. Those who continue to engage in special interest politics rather than representing the taxpayer will pay a price.

Our ideas are not offered as a panacea. In fact, they may be little more than a tourniquet for the financial hemorrhage. What New York State government requires is a zero budgeting mechanism in which every agency must justify its purpose and where expenses are routinely examined and assessed.

Mario Cuomo began his third term as governor of New York in January 1991 with an austere inaugural, forswearing the 19-gun salute and symphony overtures of four years ago. In the following months, he led the rhetorical charge for budget cuts in the face of a $6 billion deficit. He engaged in a national speaking tour to bash the Bush Administration for a "growing underclass, a deteriorating infrastructure, and a softening of our economic strength." He told the *Los Angeles*

Times, "We have a federal deficit so large people can't even remember its size and we have never been weaker economically."

The pot is not only calling the kettle black, it is claiming to be lily-white to boot. And in 1994 he unashamedly pretends he's a supply-sider. Cuomo bears primary responsibility for that $5 billion annual deficit, and for the accompanying destruction of the New York economy.

Let us recall that in his first two terms, Mr. Cuomo added 31,000 new employees to the state workforce, now numbering about 271,000. Spending rose at two and a half times the rate of inflation, while tax revenues increased by "only" 89 percent, and New York had the 47th slowest rate of job creation in the U.S. Cuomo is fond of referring to his two tax cuts (actually forced on him by the legislature), but never mentions the $1.37 in tax increases for every dollar of tax cuts, leaving combined state and local taxes the second highest in the nation, at 16.4 percent.

Cuomo insists that he is not responsible for local taxes. But local spending in New York is largely driven by state mandates, such as the freest-spending Medicaid program in the nation. In 1991, for example, the governor reduced the state contribution to the Teachers' Pension fund, forcing municipal governments to increase property taxes by $400 million to cover the shortfall. New York has 7.2 percent of the nation's population and 15 percent of the nation's accumulated debt. The debt in the state doubled under Cuomo, but that didn't stop him from blaming Washington for New York's troubles nearly forty times in his hour-long State of the State address in 1992.

The federal money stopped coming in three years ago when the boom ended, but the governor kept spending. To meet three consecutive "revenue shortfalls," the governor relied on tax increases, deficit notes, new fees, one-shot borrowing,refinancing, fund raids and a variety of sleight-of-hand accounting measures. Credit agencies took note, and the state's bond rating plummeted to third worst in the nation, ahead of only Louisiana and Massachusetts. Cuomo's response was to make a virtue of necessity. In the 1992 budget address, he proclaimed: "I will reject any proposed tax increases...any cash manipulations...the idea of deficit notes." He did not explain why he embraced these gimmicks for years, nor, in saying that it was "time for the truth," did he explain why the truth had to wait two terms before coming out.

It should thus come as no surprise that what Mario Cuomo calls "deep and painful" spending cuts are actually spending increases -i.e., cuts in projected increases.

The governor justified the cuts to his liberal followers by noting that "While these cuts are painful they must be viewed in the context of the overall generous investments of this administration in education, social service, and local aid over the last eight years." What he has not been able to show is how this reckless spending improved education, social services, or local conditions. Education spending increases of over 100 percent have been followed by drops in SAT scores (from 1980 to 1990 New York fell from 6th to 14th place among 22 states that administer the SAT), and the high school graduation rate declined from 63.4 percent in 1982 to 62.3 percent in 1988. The governor plans to cut the most expensive welfare system in America by, in the words of his budget director, "targeting benefits to the most needy." How many states need to change their welfare policies to do that? Shouldn't that have been the target all along?

When he isn't blaming Washington, Cuomo blames the state legislature for his fiscal problems. And yet he has used the line-item veto sparingly, trimming only $81 million in his first two terms. By contrast, his predecessor, Hugh Carey, a self-described liberal Democrat, cut over $1.3 billion through line-item vetoes from 1980 to 1982 alone. During Carey's two terms in the stagflation era, the proportion of New Yorkers' personal income used for state spending dropped from 9.1 to 8.6 percent. Under Cuomo, it has risen to 9.4 percent.

As he shadowboxes with the press corps in coming months, Cuomo can be expected to brag, as he did at the National Press Club in December of 1991, about his ability to make "tough decisions." If he had been willing to make those tough decisions these last twelve years, New York would not be in its present financial predicament.

As we travel around New York State, people invariably ask if the economic slide in the state's fortunes can be reversed. While it may be fashionable to discuss apocalypse, the anxiety expressed by New Yorkers is different in degree from anything we've heard in the past. Lest this mood of fear remain unchallenged, we are prepared to defend a scenario in which New York can recover and perhaps even regain the grandeur associated with its past. But our vision can only occur if the following prescriptions are entertained:

• The state's Medicaid expenditures must be controlled by calibrating service options - which at the moment are extremely generous - to private sector health plans and deregulating hospitals. Similarly, welfare dependency must be reduced through workfare and stringent eligibility requirements;

• The introduction of a voucher plan for the schools should be introduced, not only to reduce expenditures, but to provide for competition among public, private and parochial schools;

• Reducing the state's workforce is essential if the budget is to be brought under control. Consolidation of agencies, attrition and elimination of patronage and superfluous positions are most certainly warranted;

• Eliminating state economic development programs which depend on discredited public works activity and subventions for politically favored groups;

• Privatizing state and city assets such as Stewart Airport, as well as numerous administrative functions;

• Applying a means test for tuition payment at the State University;

• Eliminating state mandates on local government which force communities to raise taxes in order to meet onerous agency requirements;

• Cut state, personal and corporate tax rates dramatically to encourage business development, new investment and job creation;

• Introduce the death penalty as a symbol of society's desire for order and justice;

• Introduce mandatory sentencing in the criminal justice system so that there is certainty of punishment. Along with this reform, the construction of modular prisons at a reasonable cost and the elimination of amenities in maximum security facilities which escalate cost, must also be considered;

• Use random drug testing as a prerequisite for a drivers' license in the state, since anyone who tests positive for drugs is a menace to himself and others.

While these reforms are only the beginning of an urgently needed statewide program, they can begin to restore some confidence in the state economy, offer some hope that the streets can be reclaimed by decent citizens, and provide a reasonable level of assurance that state expenditures and taxes will be harnessed.

If the state continues to adopt business-as-usual approaches, the road to despair is inevitable. New York is choking under the pressure of debt and a correspondingly weak bond rating. Only "one-shots" and other questionable financial practices, such as selling the N.Y. State Thruway back to the state, allow the governor to meet a mandated balanced budget requirement. The net effect of these practices has been to mortgage New York's future.

At the moment, New York has both a bleak future and dismal present. The Cuomo administration has no concrete vision of what must be achieved and offers little in the way of resourceful new programs. The playwright Franz Kafka said, "There is always hope, but not for us." New Yorkers are not so cynical. We believe there is hope for us, but only if we adopt reforms which allow New Yorkers to remember why this state was once electric with opportunity and optimistic about the future. What follows is not an effort to elaborate on policy proposals mentioned in this outline, nor is this simply a critique of the policies of three Cuomo administrations. Instead, an effort has been made to discuss New York's fiscal plight with those on the frontlines, i.e. elected officials, former officials, and appointees. It is our belief that wherever one stands on the political spectrum, a consensus for reform is emerging. Both Democrats and Republicans are converging on the requisite strategy for change.

If there is a profound point this book makes it is the assertion that New York's problems and potential solutions transcend partisan politics as conventionally understood, and take us down a path of commonsensical belief that you can't spend what you don't have, and that the retrenchment proposed here need not have an adverse effect on the delivery of important services.

1 Interview: Herman Badillo

HL: One of the great concerns in New York is how to fund both the city university and the state university systems. Since you serve on the board, I wondered if we can address this question to you. The other day, Ed and I chatted with Dick Netzer. Dick said the most sensible thing to do in this state is to charge the real tuition and if people can't afford it they will not pay, but if they can afford it they would pay the real tuition instead of the present subsidized tuition. In the city university that might not generate any revenues but in the state university it might.

HB: Well, I don't think that's going to happen but clearly we have a deficit for New York State which is big and continuing to grow. But what has happened, is that when the City University had high standards, no one ever touched tuition. When open admissions was approved in 1969 the constituency that the City university had, which was primarily the Jewish community, walked away. And then City University lost its political constituency. When the fiscal crisis came about in 1974 and 1975 and one of the conditions that Congress imposed was increased tuition in the City University, there was no one fighting against it. There wasn't any constituency to keep that from happening. Tuition increase was imposed, and as the fiscal crisis got worse, the pressure to increase tuition increase. What has happened is that the City University has become another state agency, so that in the past few years when the governor had to make cuts, he made cuts which included the City University, and made up for cuts by increasing tuition. So we've had tuition increases in each of the past three years. In the next budget the same thing will happen. Once the governor found that when he imposed the $200 increase in 1991, there was no outcry, and he imposed a $500 increase this year and there was no outcry from either the alumni association or from the students, he figured he could balance the budget with tuition increases.   And that is what will happen, because there is nobody in Albany at the governor's level or at the level of the legislature, who really cares about the City University. The legislators are primarily obsessed with getting back their Members Items, their 'no-questions-asked' grants. Their first priority is not the City University. Therefore I don't see that the trend of last three years is going to change in any significant way.

HL: What do you think will happen to the City University in the future?

HB: Eventually there may have to be some closings at some campuses, but they're minor.   I don't see the governor and the legislature mandating that campuses be closed, nor are they going to eliminate all funding of the City University. They'll just cut it down proportionately. Whatever the cuts are next year, City University will take its share. This is devastating since a huge percentage of the professors and adjunct professors went through an early retirement deal this year. The City University can't go through it again, unless, when young professors see what's going on, they'll be reluctant to go there, they'll figure that the tenure track lines aren't going to be available.

HL: I can't comment non the City University, with which I'm not so familiar, but in the case of the State University, when Cuomo took office in 1983 there were 440,000 students with a budget of $2 billion. Today the budget is $4.4 billion and the student population is 350,000. Now that's a loss of 90,000 students, and more than a doubling of the budget. Something is not right; you've added 5,400 administrators in the State University in a ten year period at a time when you've lost 90,000 students. I'm not saying that 5,400 administrators account for all the increases and expenditures, and it's also true that there's been some inflation in that period, but inflation wasn't more than 100 percent. Something is wrong in the way in which we're conducting business.

HB: In the City University it's the other way around. Enrollment has increased, this year we went over 200,000, so that's the reverse problem. And we expect that we'll increase even more.

ER: Will open admissions ever be overturned? Is that politically possible? Wouldn't that be one solution, simply to allow fewer people to enter the university?

HB: It's not going to be overturned unless the governor and the mayor take a stand on it and they're not going to do that. The trustees are not going to lead the parade. Let's face it, we have a legal fiction, there's no such thing as independent trustees. Trustees are appointed by the governor and the mayor. Unless they get direction, they're not going to do anything so drastic as to eliminate open admissions. The governor or the mayor this year proposed a $500 increases and whatever the governor or the mayor propose is basically what will happen. The trustees are not going to rebel against the people who appointed them. That's not likely in the CUNY, or SUNY or the Board of Education, or Health and Hospitals Corporations. All of these legal fictions that are created as independent agents are not. The people who are appointed respond to anything the governor or the mayor says. Maybe one or two rebel, but the majority rebelling -- no way. Leadership has to come from the governor and the mayor otherwise it will never happen.

HL: Some of the states and cities have introduced means tests for their students, that is, tuition is calibrated to the earning capacity of parents, or the kids themselves. That might make sense here if those who come from families earning $20,000 pay nothing at all, and you had a scale related to the earning capacity of either the parents or the kids. Now an initiative of that kind could conceivably fly in a Democratic dominated city, because you could use the issue of equity and fairness.

HB: Maybe, as I said, maybe the mayor could do that. The best example I could give you is the case of Leonard Jeffries. This past year Professor Jeffries attacked white people, specifically Jews, and the governor and the mayor say "you shouldn't do that" but nobody gets excited and most of the trustees voted with the administration to keep Jeffries. It took about 9 months to reverse the whole thing and then, only because there were so many other problems in City College, you know with people dying at the rock concert. There is not going to be any great leadership that I can see coming out of the trustees. I'm there so I know.

HL: In the matter of Jeffries, what I don't understand is when the incident arose with his outrageous comments, you could interpret academic freedom in a kind of latitudinarian way, and say "after all, Jeffries is free to say what he wants." But there's no reason Jeffries had to retain his position as Chairman of the Black Studies Department. His position exists at the behest of the president; the president could have unilaterally or with the trustees, said "we don't want you to be chairman anymore, I'm sorry you no longer have that position."

HB: That's what I said, that was my view. But I couldn't get the trustees to go along with it, including Jewish trustees like Stanley Fink, who was the Speaker of the Assembly. The attitude was, as most of them said, if we do that, there may be riots; everybody got panicky. But if there are going to be riots, let's get it out of the way now; we can't run a university on the basis of fear of riots. I said there aren't going to be any riots, and as it turned out, there weren't any when he was fired from the post.

ER: I guess my problem with the graduated tuition scale is that --

HB: By the way, I don't approve of that either.

HL: I'm proposing it.

ER: I know, I'm just expanding the analysis a little.

HB: The reality of what's going on is that nobody really wants to affect the system. As far as I can tell, the City University is going downhill, and the legislators let it go downhill. They're not going to work for it. It's not a passionate issue with them. And there's no constituency for it; we have lost a Jewish generation. After all, we now have nearly 1400 CEOs as heads of major corporations who are graduates of City College and City University. More than Harvard or Yale. They are assets, but they have lost interest.

ER: There's no allegiance.

HB: There's no allegiance and it's not like trying to change Harvard or Yale where the graduates will really get at you. There, the trustees hear it from alumni members, their phones will really be ringing. Phones aren't ringing here from any graduates who are CEOs. And in the meantime, there are not very many black and Puerto Rican and hispanic graduates who have become heads of major corporations, so that a new constituency has developed. We lost the old crowd, we have not picked up a new crowd.

ER: Look, if you imposed open admissions on Harvard, I'm sure they'd lose their constituency as well. The idea of a university is that there is some criteria that you have to fall into in order to become a member of that club.

HB: But there's nobody who cares. The tactic, designed by the governor is very clever. By giving the legislators Member Items, which I thought was not a smart thing to do because it really is a payoff,he's got them hostage because with the budget cuts, he can say "look, you guys want to restore money to CUNY or do you want money for the Member Items?" They take the Member Items.

HL: They're captives.

HB: They're totally captives. And they will admit privately if not publicly that their first priority is Member Items.

ER: Getting elected.

HB: Yes, getting elected. Much as they would like to help you, they have got to look out for their own behind. And that means you've got to get the Member Items first. So the political situation is such that everybody is roped in.

HL: Well, it's a very sad state of affairs but I think you've stated it very accurately. Anything you want to add?

ER: Would you like to comment on the general effect of the NYS public school system on CUNY?

HB: The NYC public school system is the main disaster because (former) Chancellor Fernandez admits that fewer than 20 percent of the students graduating from high school have a meaningful diploma. You get phoney diplomas. Very few actually graduate from high school anyway, but those who do cannot read or write or speak, and the reason

for that is that in the educational system everybody passes, no one
flunks. I keep saying over and over that when I came here from Puerto
Rico I thought America was very strange, because in Puerto Rico if you
did your work you passed and if you didn't, you flunked. Here, if you
do your work you pass if you don't do your work you pass. It's called
by a technical name: social promotion, which is just another excuse for
not wanting to face up to disciplining the system.

Some educators say that it's sociologically bad for a child to be left
behind; therefore he should be moved along with his peers even if he's
not learning. I said o.k., show me the sociologist who wrote the book.
There is no sociologist, nobody ever wrote such a book because it's a
stupid idea. It is sociologically worse for a child to be seventeen years
old and not be able to read or write or speak, and you don't need a
sociologist to tell you that. But everybody gets kicked upstairs and they
go into CUNY, into the community colleges, or one of the other
programs. Some students spend years getting a regular high school
diploma, but most are passed along.

Now, CUNY Chancellor Ann Reynolds has come up with a program
that's called The College Preparatory Initiative, which I voted for. It
mandates the Board of Education, within a certain number of years, to
graduate students who have earned a real high school diploma, which
includes a certain number of years of English, algebra and science,
among other things. The problem is that Joe Fernandez said, "I love
that idea but give me the money for it, because if I'm going to provide
these courses I've got to have more teachers and I've got to train them
and there's no money for it." Therefore it's just whistling in the wind.
And the College Preparatory Initiative says if the kids so not meet the
requirements they're allowed to come in anyway. So there's no need
for it; it's just political fencing.

ER: With open admissions what difference does it make?

HB: That's right. It doesn't abolish open admissions, does it?

ER: I think you made a very interesting point in the interview that you
had in the *City Journal*, that before open admissions there was great
pressure from CUNY to hone the public school system. I guess there
was a great pressure from people who had their kids in the public
school system to give them a curriculum that would enable them to be

admitted to CUNY. But now that's a moot point because everybody gets in. They're losing a lot of energy in the public schools because of open admissions.

HB: And the people at CUNY say "well, we do have standards, because you can get into a community college with nothing, but you need an eighty percent average to get into senior colleges." But an eighty percent average from Morris High School doesn't mean anything because there are no standards there, but an eighty percent average from Bronx Science is something else.

HL: Since standards have been vitiated it's understandable that what you're talking about is circular. Why should anyone have allegiance to a system that doesn't have any standards? Why should the high schools be preparing people to engage in rigorous work when they can get into the college program without rigorous work? And why should Mr. Fernandez change the curriculum and put teachers through some sort of training program when in fact it really doesn't mean anything to the teachers or the students. So you've got a system that is really corrupted and it's very cruel - if the things that you say are really true, and I believe they are, there really isn't any justification for the retention of the City University. In fact one can argue that what the legislators are doing in letting the system fall by the wayside is the appropriate thing to do.

HB: That's what's going on, that's exactly what's happening. My view, I'm one of a few trustees who believes in having rigorous standards; I told you at the beginning I voted against open admissions in 1969 when I was running for mayor. I haven't changed my point of view since then. Precisely for the reason you give, that it destroys the whole concept, it destroyed City University and it destroyed any incentive in the public school system. And we have to really come back to imposing standards. Without standards in education a whole generation is lost. The worst part of it is that most black and hispanic parents don't know this. Their kids get a report card that says they passed everything, so they figure they passed because in the countries where they come from you don't pass automatically. Then they find out the kids can't read and they're furious. And the kids, of course, don't really know what they're supposed to be learning.

HL: But you say the parents are furious and I suspect you're right, but where is the political manifestation of that fury?

HB: These parents don't have any political clout. They're not like middle class parents who will follow the kids to school. Poor people are overwhelmed by the struggle to keep the family together, such as it is, or to pay the rent or to get food, so that they really cannot cope with the bureaucracy of the public school system, or the bureaucracy of the hospital system, or emergency rooms of hospitals. The average poor person doesn't know a family doctor, doesn't have a dentist, has no idea how to get a dentist. When there's a crisis and an appendix is bursting or they're about to give birth, they go to the emergency room of a hospital. So in that kind of family, the kid is going to school without guidance. The principal doesn't call the parents in and there are generally no complaints. Don't forget, many of the parents themselves don't have an education, so you can't ask them to supervise something that they never did themselves.

HL: I was quite interested when Rev. Reuben Diaz wanted to organize a demonstration against condom distribution in NYC public school system. I saw 12,000 people at 110 Livingston Street, most of them hispanics.

HB: Yes, because condom distribution polarizes the city. Things like that polarize, like the civilian review board. But I'm not talking about one-shot demonstrations. When you can get 200 ministers to turn out their people, you can get a big crowd for one day. But I'm not talking about a one-shot thing; day to day monitoring of where the kid is going is something poor people can't do. In many of the countries, especially in Central American countries, there's no tradition of education. For example in Guatemala, there is no public educational system. The Indians are not encouraged to get an education, because the Spaniards control the system don't want the Indians educated, so they've never had a tradition of public education. Therefore it's unreasonable to expect them to come here and want an education when there is no tradition of education or learning.

HL: You presented a very interesting picture of education in the city and we thank you for your time. It's also a rather depressing picture.

HB: Yes, you need leadership at the top. Unless you have it, everybody wants to cover up. Unless you get someone who cares passionately about change, nothing happens. (Former Mayor) Dinkins says he wants to be an education mayor but he's as much an education mayor as Bush was an education president, because Dinkins cut the budget for the community colleges. I have to fight just to get the budget restored for John Jay and the technical colleges.

ER: Is there any constituency for going back to the pre-1969 period?

HB: That has to be a decision made by the governor and the mayor if it is made, at all, by top leadership, then it can be secured. But in the absence of that, teachers aren't going to rock the boat. I mean, believe it or not, the majority of the faculty at City College who are Jewish supported Jeffries for the chairmanship of the Black Studies Department.

HL: They thought it was politically correct I'm sure that it was consistent with prevalent attitudes.

HB: Some professors don't want to get involved. They will complain to me, they'll come in here or send me letters, but they don't want their names used.

ER: I know the Jewish professor who was adamantly against Jeffries, he's a sociologist, Steven Goldberg, the token conservative, I guess on the faculty.

HB: But the majority voted for Jeffries. So you don't have a constituency even within the university for change. And the teachers don't want to get involved and the UFT lives in terror that black and Puerto Rican parents are going to go after them and they need cover from the top. If the mayor were to take a stand, fine. But in the absence of that, bureaucracies are not going to change on their own.

HL: Thank you very much.

Commentary: HL

At what point do subsidies undermine the very institutions they were designed to promote? In economic terms, when you subsidize an institution so that its fee is nowhere near market rates, you degrade the service and create an environment in which the service isn't valued. For several generations of New Yorkers who attended City College as a rite of passage leading to a professional career, the effects of subsidies were ignored. New Yorkers took pride in *their* great college without much attention to the actual cost.

After 1969, when open admissions was approved, a change in attitude was introduced as well. College students were now subsidized to engage in remedial level work that could not be dignified as a secondary school standard. At this point the political influence of City College diminished as did the argument for continued subsidies.

For many black New Yorkers who were the primary beneficiaries of open admissions the change in attitude was *prima facie* evidence of a racial standard. For alumni who adhered to a meritocratic view of the university, open admissions was the opening salvo in a war to degrade all standards of performance. The disparity between present student views and alumni views is widening and irreconcilable. There is little political capital in overturning the open admissions policy and little that can be done to appease alumni members estranged from the institution that once nurtured them. As Herman Badillo notes the City University is adrift, with neither mayor nor governor willing to address the central questions of what should this university system provide, for whom and at what cost.

In the face of a volatile political climate, the path of least resistance is incrementalism. The mandate is to do something insignificant that doesn't mobilize the dissidents, even if what is done doesn't satisfy any constituency. As a consequence, the muscle for genuine political action atrophies. Herman Badillo notes that the recent Leonard Jeffries incident was a manifestation of political cowardice. It wasn't until the ineffectiveness of the City College administration was painfully evident that any action regarding Jeffries' appointment was taken (the decision to remove Jeffries from his departmental chair was reversed in the courts.)

Since the trustees of City University are appointed by the governor, and since legislators who argue for additional funding can be held hostage to "Member Items"--grants given directly to legislators from the governor and leader of each house, and which do not go through a legislative process--a voice for reform of the university system doesn't exist or is easily modulated. Moreover, Mr. Badillo points out that the public school system which is the principal feeder for the university is in thralldom to a radical egalitarianism that fears failure more than incompetent students. The result is that students who do not possess college level skills are still inserted into a college environment that similarly creates the illusion that everyone is deserving of a degree.

It is ironic that the University Chancellor's College Preparatory Initiative, which mandates a certain number of "real" subjects as high school graduation requirement, was challenged by the Chancellor of the City School System who alleged more money was needed in order to introduce this plan, and challenged as well by proponents of open admissions who contend that any standard violates the spirit of the open admission policy.

By allowing the University to vitiate standards, a cancer cell has metastasized throughout New York's educational institutions. For decades, a letter of acceptance from a university was more important than a high school diploma. It suggested that a university admissions officer considered you worthy of college level study. But what is one to make of an acceptance letter which doesn't employ any standard of intellectual discrimination? In this case, the work one does as a high school student is meaningless, as is educational attainment at every level.

One might assume, as I do, that parents would see through this charade. Yet Mr. Badillo notes that the average person is so overwhelmed with making ends meet, he doesn't truly understand what is going on in the schools. I respectfully disagree. The "choice movement" in education is largely comprised of average people who are asking why Johnny is promoted when he can't read or write. One doesn't have to possess a college degree to maintain that something is wrong with the schools. When kids can spend more time putting condoms on cucumbers than solving quadratic equations something is wrong and many parents sense it.

It isn't money alone that will restore integrity to the City University. It starts, it seems to me, with an accurate and uncompromising profile of what presently passes for higher education in the city. Unless standards are imposed from the top with a mayor and governor taking all the heat such a decision would generate, the City University will continue to flounder with vague references to a majestic distant past that fewer and fewer city residents will be able to recall.

2 Interview: Edward Costikyan

ER: Do you think Ed Koch provided an example of responsible government? I know that the city's payroll went up tremendously while he was mayor. And he said that federal aid is not always a good deal for the city.

EC: Well, yes, he did say that, but you've got to take a careful look at who Koch was running against in the primary--Bella Abzug--who was for the federal government to solve every problem. Ed carved out a niche in which city self-reliance to solve problems was the key ingredient. And he believed that. He also believed that was the way he would win the primary. And you've got to remember that Ed was subject to constraints. He wasn't a free agent, he couldn't rely on the federal government. He had the Financial Control Board approving everything he did, or disapproving, and he knew that.

HL: But if you go back to 1975, when the Financial Control Board was introduced, largely as a result of the crisis in New York, it took a crisis to bring about that change. Do we have to be at the precipice of despair before introducing appropriate reforms, or is it possible to get a mandate for reform using a campaign?

EC: I don't think you can get a mandate for reform using a campaign unless there's a crisis. I don't think you can get the attention of the voters. They're not that interested in government; they never have been. We look back and say, there was a day when everybody voted but there was never a day when everybody voted. There was a day when there was a turnout of 60, 70, 80 percent. Those people weren't voting because of their deep interest in what was happening; they were voting because they had a political relationship with the party on the local level, and somebody came and rang their doorbell and said "today is election day." And the friendly voter would ask, "Who are we for today?" And the captain would tell them who the party was supporting. There wasn't this great knowledge, although there was probably some knowledge about government because our educational system made an effort to teach kids something called civics which is no longer taught. I don't know how much people learned from that course, I never took it. I went to a private school where they taught us history and other things that allowed us to learn something about government. But I think even in those days you got citizen interest when there was a crisis.

ER: But wasn't there the perception that government worked back then and it doesn't work today?

EC: And it did work then.

ER: It did fewer things but it did them well.

EC: It did fewer things, and some of the things it's doing now, if you had suggested doing thirty years ago, you would have been laughed at. Condoms in schools? I mean, sure it's a serious problem, and it ought to be dealt with. You're going to have teachers performing this role? It would have been laughed out of town. I don't know how you get back to that era though, because you've got to start with an education system that instills in young people the notion that civics is important and that's hard to do when it really looks like it isn't.

HL: Absolutely. It's hard to know what you can count on in politics.

EC: Did Dan Quayle use family pressure influence to get elected? I know the answer to that question and so do you. And so do the American people, but I don't think they care about it. How do you get the issues, the New York State issues, before the people? I don't know. I don't think they're going to pay attention to them until there's a crisis. And I think we're close to a crisis.

HL: Well, if you look at the bond rating in New York, it is now the lowest in the United States. We have that distinction. The other interesting fact is that New York City went beyond one million people on welfare.

EC: We were there once before.

HL: That's right, I think it was in the early sixties.

EC: I remember it was a shock.

HL: I think that sent shock waves through this political system.

ER: But that was a different situation back then, that was the start of the Great Society. People were gearing up for the welfare state and this was perceived as a temporary phenomenon. They were signing people up only to get them off in a fairly brief amount of time.

EC: New York City was then having an economic decline and the huge welfare numbers were a byproduct of that. Nobody thought it was acceptable.

HL: Nobody thought it was a permanent condition. I think the attitude today is quite different. I think people believe that the number one million is temporary, and that we'll see a million and a half in the not too distant future.

EC: I don't know how you focus public attention on what the state is doing. Part of it is the extension of state mandates in the last ten years. This is an easy, cheap way, for the state to say, "look what we've done" but the state doesn't have to pay for what it has done, the localities do, and nobody reacts to that.

HL: Well localities are driven to the state of despair. You've destroyed local communities in this state. Little towns, like Glen Falls, are being driven out of existence. They can't survive. Because they have either of two choices: raise the sales tax, or raise the property taxes. Either one is unpalatable.

EC: How much of the local budgets is a product of mandated expenses?

HL: In some counties as much as 70 percent.

EC: I always thought that one way to deal with this was to adopt a constitutional amendment or a law that says, the state can't impose a duty on a municipality unless it pays for it itself.

ER: California has done that.

HL: California has done that and New York now has precisely that proposal. A change in the state constitution to allow municipalities to decide whether or not it will accept mandates. Bob King, county executive in Monroe County, in Rochester, is the author.

EC: It's a good idea but it will knock the hell out of the state budget. But you know, there's another aspect to this, and that is, what recourse does a citizen have with a legislature that runs the way ours does? I don't want to be publicly critical of it because I represented it on numerous occasions. Yet the way the state legislature functions makes it almost impossible to raise this kind of an issue. It's much easier for the legislator to say, when he comes back to run for re-election, "I enacted a law that does thus-and-so." It looks good, and it is good, and it was probably a valid, worthwhile purpose, but who paid for it? I think you have a real rough problem to make this a demonstrable proposition for voters. I don't know whether you can do it short of a crisis.

HL: Surely the idea of state taxes, which now represent something on the order of 17 percent of one's wealth, is a factor in the creation of an issue. It was one thing when you were talking about 10 percent of one's wealth.

EC: I don't think voters make that kind of calculation. I think voters get used to the level of taxation, whatever it is. And then it goes up a little, and they expect that, and they get used to that.

ER: But then their job vanishes.

EC: That's when it becomes a factor. When the job vanishes--they are vanishing all over. I have a paper here called "The Era of Fundamental Stalemate and the Possibility of a Long Reconstructive Revolution in America", by Gar Alperovitz. He's a radical, and I don't agree with some of his arguments. But what he is saying here is that the rate of unemployment in this country has been going up dramatically over the

last 30 years. An average 4.8 percent in the '50s, 4.8 percent in the
'60s, 6.2 in the '70s, 7.8 in the 80's, and we're creating a society with
a large number of unemployables.

ER: Well I should write a rebuttal to Mr. Alperovitz. Because there's
a good reason for that. It's not that the economy is falling out of bed.
The fraction of people working today is higher than it ever was before.
They measure unemployment by the people who are looking for a job--

EC: I always thought that was phony--

ER: It is. As a percent of people who are in the labor force, people
who don't have jobs versus those who do. There are so many people
who want work now because they know it's available. I mean
historically, over the last 30 years the percentage of people who are
either working or looking for work, has gone up tremendously.

HL: But New York City is in a different state, New York City is in a
very unusual condition.

EC: I think the state is too.

HL: We've lost 575,000 jobs since the recession began four years ago.
And that represents 40 percent of the jobs lost in the nation over that
time; 375,000 jobs were lost in the city during this same period.

EC: In the city, that's the number I saw.

HL: That's Steve Kagann's statistic, and I think that is a demonstration
of the weakness in the New York economy. That is due in part to the
tax problem that we're facing. We're driving private capital out of
existence.

EC: It's much easier to go someplace where it's cheaper to do
business. But I don't know how that gets translated into jobs. I have
a hunch that one of the reasons why this has not been translated into the
electoral process is that the Republicans, in all respects, have not run
significant candidates, even my friend with the red suspenders, Lew
Lehrman. Lew didn't have the credentials to be a serious candidate
and I think part of the reason was his obsession with talking about the

gold standard, which made absolutely no sense to anyone.

HL: Still, Lehrman came within 2 percent of victory. And if I had the Republican nomination, assuming I would have had Rinfret's vote, which is a rock-bottom Republican vote, I would have been within 6 points of winning the governorship. So, I think it can be won by a Republican.

EC: I understand what you're saying. It may be, but I don't think the current leadership in the party has the capacity to come up with a candidate who can do it and come up with enough time to make the case. It would take a year of work to start spreading this word throughout the state, using the techniques of modern communication and doing it deliberately.

HL: But suppose you're on the other side. Suppose you're running a Democratic campaign, not necessarily for Mario Cuomo. How would you tell him to run the campaign, what advice would you give him? How would you prepare him to be the next governor of New York?

EC: I would tell him what I told Koch. You can't rely on the federal government, you've got to do it yourself, we've got to cut back, you've got to reduce the size of government. I was the source of the Koch assault on unions and on public sector pensions, which we couldn't afford if they continued to grow. We made some progress on the pensions, but not as much as I thought we should. Today, to get elected, I would say you need a machine that's running full steam ahead and I think you've got to start a year ahead, you've got to start laying out why it's costing so much to do so little. I would say let's start with the five major areas of cost to which people are sensitive. I would start probably with education, which has just gone up sky high, even though I don't think teachers are paid enough.

HL: Well, I agree with you. But it's costing $8500 to educate a kid in the New York public schools. When I went to Columbia college, the tuition was $750 a year.

EC: When I started it was $400. It's now $20,000 a year for tuition and books and living expenses. How did that happen? I know how it happened at Columbia. First of all, academicians were not well paid by modern standards. But they had not been badly paid in the Depression years, and that sort of laid the base. The second is that they taught a lot more and spent less time on research. The teaching load, when I was at Columbia College, for a full professor or anybody else, was 12 hours a week, unless he was the head of a department or had some administrative duty--then it was nine. The faculty also did the advising; every student had a faculty advisor. They also did the committee work; they conceived the curriculum, and that took time. They watched it and they supervised it. Today, the average teaching role is 6 hours one semester and 3 hours another. The advising function is handled by other people and whatever curriculum work they do, I think is subtracted from the teaching hours. Well, if you cut the number of hours that you're putting into teaching by 50 percent, you've got to double the number of faculty members to teach the same number of students. I don't know what the cost problems are in the education system now, because I haven't really looked at it. I did in the 1970's, and it was obvious that the schools were overloaded with administrators. I remember there was a bureau of new school construction even though a new school hadn't been built in New York City in five years. They had all these guys sitting down and worrying about new school construction.

The other bureaucracy I remember was the licensing process, through the Board of Examiners. The city procedure was created before the state had adequate standards. After the state created standards, there was no need for New York City to have a separate set, especially since we weren't getting better teachers than Suffolk County or Nassau County. I don't know the extent to which that has continued, but I think it has. I would think that if somebody wanted to go after these excesses they should say, okay let's look at the five major areas of expenditure and then let's really rip apart why it costs $8000 per student. Is that money getting to the teachers? It isn't. My mother was a teacher; she taught at Horace Mann School, which was a private school. I once asked her, 'Mom, how come you never wanted to go into the public school system?' She said there are two reasons. One was that she was educated in Switzerland and didn't have a college degree that would enable her to teach in a public school; the second reason was that the public schools have all kinds of things like teaching plans, and study plans, and reports and she said nobody bothers me here with that nonsense, they just let me teach kids how to speak French. Well, that's got to be part of the problem, too. We're trying to manage this school system and we're over managing it; we've got too many managers.

ER: Well again, the state has its finger in that pot too.

EC: Sure it does. The department of education is a monster of a bureaucracy. If you've ever had any dealings with it, you can never get it to do anything because they have too many people to consult. But that's where your dollar goes. The teachers are underpaid, but the whole system is overfinanced. The people want good schools, they really do, they're just frustrated that they're not getting it. The teachers' union has been very effective in saying give us more--we need more money because the schools need more. Well the schools need more money if it gets to the right place but as I see it you can cut the budget substantially and not affect the quality of education. I can think of a half dozen examples of substantial unnecessary costs. But this has to be translated into something you can take to the people and say "this is affecting you," and "this is why you're not getting what you should be getting." A candidate could do that, but not in two months. It's got to be a long period of cultivation.

ER: You think school choice is an issue that resonates with parents? I don't think it is, not in this city.

EC: I think the Manhattan Institute version of it is resonating within the districts that have it. It had a good impact on the teachers. I don't think the choice is between public and private schools. Parents think if I can get my children into a private school and can afford it, I'll pay for it. Catholic schools are in a different position because they're not for upper income families.

HL: That may be the central argument. It's not really a public/ private dichotomy or a parochial/public dichotomy. It's a matter of giving parents real choices.

EC: I think that the concern about separation of church and state, which I grew up with and I'm sure you did too, is no longer as strong as it was. I've always thought that someone could make an awfully good case for the proposition that schools don't teach religion, they're teaching people how to function and do a good job of it, at a lot less cost. It is a good investment. The fear of the Catholic Church taking over the United States is kind of silly.

HL: Yes, I guess we've passed through the Nativist surge in the 19th Century.

EC: After Kennedy and Cuomo, the country has changed about that issue. I wouldn't have a public-private choice, but I would consider a public-parochial choice. We really don't raise this problem with Catholic hospitals, do we?

HL: St. Vincent's gets money from the government.

EC: We're happy to have it take care of sick people. I think you could get away with that. The proposal would meet some resistance but I think a candidate could get away with saying we need the two systems. Part of the reason for it is the lower cost of the Catholic schools due to more efficient management. There's some risk to the idea. But I don't know about the other issue, the health care system.

HL: The health and welfare system.

EC: Dr. Axelrod, the former state Health Commissioner, I always thought, was the product of an accountant's mind. I remember when he wanted to cut back on the hospital beds here. He cut back like crazy, as if he were saving money. He says he eliminated the beds, and lowered the cost, but he didn't. He just changed the computation. He took hospitals with excess beds and cut them out of the system, creating a shortage again. The end result is that on the northern end of Manhattan there is only one public hospital now, Columbia Presbyterian. And it doesn't have the public funds to carry it. Presbyterian almost went under about three years ago. He also had strange notions about MRIs, Magnetic Resonant Imaging.

Dr. Axelrod had access and control over seven MRI centers. He was going to license them to hospitals in New York State. We represented Sloan Kettering then. One of my partners called me up and asked, "Do you know how to get to the Commissioner of Health?" I said "no," and he said "You've got to get to him. He's going crazy." I asked, "what's he doing?" "He's saying he's going to give one of these MRIs to New York Hospital and he's not going to give one to

Sloan Kettering." And I said, "well he only has seven." My partner said, "I know, but we've said we'd buy our own. And we won't put it in the base costs." The machine cost a million dollars. I reached Dr. Axelrod and he was intransigent. He said the people from Sloan Kettering can take the patients across to New York Hospital using a tunnel under the street. There's a tunnel between the two hospitals. I said, "Commissioner, they can take patients there, but New York Hospital will let the S.K. physicians use the machine only three hours a week." Dr. Axelrod remained intransigent and was later overruled by his board. That was the way he directed health policies. I don't know why anyone hasn't taken a look at what emanated from that office. It was certainly not cost effective. I'm sure there is far too much supervision of medical services. You trust doctors with a knife on the operating table, but you don't trust them to have any judgment about anything else.

ER: An interesting point about the hospitals is that I did a paper on Medicaid in New York. I compared it with California where they have a much less expensive program, although actually treating more people and spending less, about $2 billion less than New York does. California had the hospitals compete for the state Medicaid contracts. The New York people said, we can't do that because there's no vacancy rate in New York, the hospitals are totally utilized. Where are we going to put more patients? So you come full circle. The reason they're utilized is because there's state restriction on this matter.

EC: I don't think hospitals are full. The Health and Hospitals Corporation has got to be a sponge for money. The problem has got to be translated into something the electors will understand. Its very hard to comprehend in the abstract. Does anyone know how much Cuomo has increased the state budget? How much he's increased the annual deficit?

HL: Oh, I think I know the answers to those questions.

EC: Yes but does the public know?

HL: I don't think anyone has the slightest idea. In fact, I find it rather amusing because as you know California had its recent crisis when the governor tried introducing some retrenchment into the California budget.

But the problems associated with the budget deficit in New York are much worse than California.

EC: But their problem was apparent, wasn't it?

HL: It was apparent largely because it became a political crisis, since the legislature was obviously involved in negotiations with Pete Wilson about what the cuts would be. But the fact is that we have a crisis of far greater magnitude here in New York that no one knows about.

EC: It would be a hard subject to sell, and it would take a long time to do it. You're not going to get any help from the legislature because the State Senate is part of the team. On many issues Senator Marino only does something when there's some personal, political benefit. He fouled up the redistricting plan this year because he was worried about some Democratic assemblyman running against him for state senate. Marino wanted him to run for Congress instead, against someone else. This assemblyman had no intention of running for Congress, he couldn't afford it, but he was driving Marino crazy. I think an agreement on redistricting could have been achieved but every time they were ready to sign on the bottom line, he'd raise the specter of this Democrat. Of course, you're not going to get this kind of issue raised through the normal political process, because the normal political process is not attuned to raising it.

HL: Well maybe you have to manufacture a crisis.

EC: Perhaps, but how do you do that?

HL: When the fraudulent fiscal Ponzi scheme in New York collapsed in 1975 you certainly had a crisis.

EC: That's right, but it wasn't manufactured on purpose. It just finally happened. I don't know whether we're close to that now. Are we?

HL: I think that in some respects we probably are. New York State is in Chapter 11, obviously the sale of bonds at the end of the fiscal year allowed Cuomo to balance the budget. But were it not for that, in what I call prestidigitation--taking a rabbit out of the hat--selling Route 287 to the New York Thruway Authority or selling Attica Prison to the

Urban Development Corporation, the state couldn't balance the budget.

EC: Attica Prison to the UDC. There are a lot of people turning over in their graves on account of that.

HL: It's bizarre. Who else could get away with that, except Cuomo.

ER: There is also the housing problem in New York.

EC: I don't know how you translate this concern into something doable in the political environment unless there's a real crisis, and it may be we're headed for that. It's true that if there is a crisis, it will focus the public attention just as the California crisis did. But I don't know who creates the crisis. For the city its obvious that the crisis can be created when revenues go down and expenses can't be met.

ER: Don't forget that in '75 the crisis happened in the year of a new governor. Carey was not part of the club.

EC: He wasn't.

ER: The establishment didn't like him, the bankers didn't like him.

EC: But he stepped in.

ER: Yes, he did. I think Cuomo has the political skills to prevent a crisis; he's always managed to put the pieces together, and a jerry-built budget is signed into law. That will haunt us years down the road, because obviously there's interest to be paid on this borrowing.

EC: Unfortunately, nobody worries about that anymore.

ER: Well that's true, you just pay off the interest with more bonds.

EC: Three years ago, I told an investment banker about the problem of the national debt. He said, "it's no problem at all." I said, "what do you mean it's no problem at all?" He said, "it's only a small percentage of the gross national product." I said, "that's crazy. What happens if the gross national product is static and the debt increases?"

HL: Precisely.

EC: The federal government doesn't own the gross national product.

HL: Although there are some people in the federal government who think they own the gross national product.

EC: I think it's catching up with us. What happens next year unless something is done?

HL: I can't see how the governor can continue to increase the budget by six, seven percent a year. And I can't see how he can go through another trick by selling a parking lot at Aqueduct to the highway authority. How many of those tricks are there? He sold a canal system to the New York State Thruway this year.

EC: Its just outrageous. Then they raise the tolls on the Thruway. Well this has been a very stimulating series of questions. I wish I had some insight as to how things are going to work. But I guess you're right--a crisis is what is necessary to bring home results and if somebody's going to try and make this fight he has to start early.

HL: I have taken that comment very seriously. I have started running for '94. I am out there working hard right now.

Commentary: HL

Is the electorate aware of the broad spectrum of political options on particular issues, or do they perceive them as a gaggle of impressions without any clear focus, or are they aware only of their own interest? Thomas Jefferson maintained that an uneducated people cannot sustain a democratic government. That observation is as valid now as it was when constitutional government in the United States was established. Ed Costikyan, as skillful a political professional as one can find in New York, contends that with the expansion of government authority, public officials do much more now than they ever did, but tend not to do many things well. One consequence of this increased activity is that the public's expectations for government has increased geometrically, while the actual delivery of basic services has decreased. The disparity between expectation and reality has resulted in widespread cynicism that makes it even more difficult to govern than was once the case. As the cost of government activity rises, public officials constantly seek new ways to have some other level of government pay the bills. The dramatic increase in mandates over the last fifteen years in which state authorities establish requirements that must be met by county government is an unambiguous illustration of this phenomenon. A state agency will issue an order, for example, to establish uniform social service benefits. Since the order is not accompanied by funding, localities that cannot meet the standard are obliged to either raise sales taxes or property taxes. The governor will then turn around and say "I haven't raised your taxes; it's your county or municipal government that is at fault."

This deception is having a corrosive influence on local governments in New York State, but thus far, mandate relief is little more than a topic for discussion. If, in fact, localities were to determine the level of service they can afford, the state government would have to enter the breach or take full responsibility for the failure to meet a service standard. Far better, of course, for the state to have it both ways: craft the requirement and then impose it on localities where taxes are raised to meet the requirement.

Can voter sentiments be aroused on issues like mandates? Or are the voters merely manipulated into the acceptance of legislation they rarely understand? Is the problem in politics the quality of the candidates or is there something structurally wrong with the process?

While Mr. Costikyan is a realist whose enthusiasm for city and state politics has been dampened by experience, he nonetheless advocates a campaign organized around ideas which, as he puts it, could win an election. These ideas include retrenchment of government employees and pension funds and cost containment for education. How one moves from good ideas and glib assertions to actual reductions is not clear. However, the five to six percent annual attrition rate for state employees is a major wedge for any governor. A mere freeze on state employment could reduce the state workforce by twenty percent in one term. As far as educational expenditures are concerned, it is possible to consider a voucher based on a means-tested standard of say, $45,000 or less, which would allow competition among public, private and parochial schools and, most important, serve as a demonstration that a superior education can be provided at $3000 per student instead of the

$8500 per capita expenditure now in place.

Whether a school voucher plan can be organized for New York is largely a function of the state's political calculus. Can an effective coalition be assembled that is capable of challenging the influence of the American Federation of Teachers (AFT) and the National Education Association (NEA) that are adamantly opposed to the proposal? The success of the unions in undermining the California proposition for school vouchers does not auger well for any such proposal in New York. Yet it is also clear that with educational costs rising at an undiminished rate, and property taxes going up correspondingly (75 percent of property taxes are set aside for school expenses), those people living on fixed incomes cannot pay their property taxes without "circuit breakers," which in New York State are not generous enough to make a difference. In this climate, every newspaper article which chronicles a school administrator with a $1 million "golden parachute" adds kerosene to an open fire. New Yorkers who say "I can't take it anymore" are growing; if history is any guide, they will be heard from.

When people are directly affected by government action, they can be mobilized to act. In my judgment, the expansion of state authority under the rubrics of education, environmentalism, and health care have brought many angry citizens under the tent of state regulation. Whether these people who represent different concerns but are venting anger at the same target, can be mobilized as a force for reform remains to be seen. But the catalyst for public education may be the moment one's ox is gored. As I see it, there are enough oxen being gored in New York to represent an army of disenchanted voters.

3 Interview: John Gilbert

ER: We might as well address the issue that is at the heart of the real estate problem in New York City. We know that rent control is the problem, we would like you to address it.

JG: Actually, I think what I'd like to do is start with a bigger picture. The most incredible example of what is wrong with New York today is right in front of us. You can go to Sunset Park in Brooklyn where there's a new development, there's a new Chinatown being born, it's already born, now it's growing. What's remarkable about this is the fact that Chinese, from mainland China and Hong Kong, come to Sunset Park, come to the United States; they don't speak the language, and probably have trouble exchanging their money when they first get here, figuring out the differentials. But you look at the example of Sunset Park, and here you have a new wave of immigration that's supposed to save New York, and they're coming here and they know enough not to buy rent stabilized and rent controlled properties.

If you look at the mid-blocks in this neighborhood, they'll buy up anything that's 3, 4, 5 units, but they won't touch a single building with 6 units or more. What does that tell you? It tells you a lot of things. Number one, that the dynamic that is going to save New York is opportunity, is empowerment, is the ability of people of modest means to come to New York and to make it. They are able to grow and to create a nest egg, and even more than a nest egg--a ladder for themselves and for their family so that their kids can go to college, so that their grandchildren can continue to buy property. They're coming here and investing their hard earned dollars in property that is the least regulated property you can possibly have, and staying away from property that is overregulated by either rent controls or rent stabilization. Everybody up and down the line is saying that the reason why New York is going to really grow and be saved is this new wave of immigration.

Let's go back and take a look at what happened in the early part of this century, the difference is that you don't have the same level of opportunity, the same avenues that people can walk down, the same trails, they're not there. They're much more limited. It's revealing that 60% of the membership of the association of small property owners in the city is foreign born (22,000). Most of the folks who come here are not as educated as the Chinese in Sunset Park. When they buy a building, it often doesn't turn out to be the American dream, it turns into the American nightmare. It's Pacific Heights all over again; they buy a building and are immediately bombarded with regulations and paperwork, and in many cases they can't read it. We've got multilingual counselors here who speak three dialects of Chinese, Polish, and Spanish. We're trying to get into different neighborhoods; we should get someone who speaks Russian, dialects of all the countries in the former Soviet Union. But the bottom line, the problem with New York is that today, the mayor, right on down to the city council member and right on up to the governor (in terms of what role he plays), are allowing our tax base to disappear. It's a 270% increase in the number of buildings that have been seized by the City of New York since 1988. We don't have to talk about the 1970's anymore and the 500,000 apartments that were seized by the city and lost to abandonment. We're talking today, in the last four years, a 270% increase.

Last year alone in Brooklyn, we had a 253% increase in the number of buildings seized by the City of New York. No one's doing a damn thing about it. So the problem is that the ability of this city to pay for the services that people demand, whether it's police, fire, or good schools, are just being allowed to disappear. And the sad part about it is when you lose a single building in the City of New York, you lose twice. You lose the taxes that you would have collected, and then you have to find the money to run that building that used to make money for the city. Overall, it's the unwillingness to change, and I think it's a political frame of mind, I don't think it's really ideological, I think it's political. You look at all the environmental issues that we have. What are we going to do about the shortage of water? Well, let's say it's a great idea to put a meter in every single building. What incentive does a tenant have living on the 13th floor, to conserve water, when they know that the owner is going to pay for it and they won't pay a single red cent toward the consumption of that water. They turn on the faucet, there's no connection between turning that faucet on and their pocketbook, zero. Two thirds of the city's population lives in rental housing, and yet we are in the process right now of spending millions of dollars to install water meters. That's going to do one thing, it will destroy low- and moderately-priced privately-owned housing. Gone. Finis. Bye-bye.

Look at the census data that was released today: one of the most remarkable numbers is the amount of overcrowding that we now have in our privately-owned rental housing. Interestingly enough, it is the new immigrants who are doubling up and tripling up. Not unlike the early part of the century, when the lower East Side was this incredible melting pot of people coming mostly from Europe, doubling up. Now they're coming from the Caribbean, coming from the Far East. We've lost that base of housing where these immigrants would have lived. It's gone. It's not there. You talk to owners, and I can give you names of people on the lower East Side, Chinatown and Little Italy. A guy owns a building, a very nice building occupied by Chinese. But people reside in those buildings in shifts, the shift that works through the night comes in and sleep during the day; the shift that works during the day comes in and sleep at night. His water bill went up by 500% after the meter was put in. There isn't any opportunity for him to recoup any of those dollars. That housing is going to be gone.

The problem of lead paint is another example of the risk to privately-owned housing. We are right now in the midst of an incredible hysteria over lead paint. All of us have lived with it; we go to sleep at night, if you live in a building that was built before 1960, it is surrounding you, lead paint everywhere. The difference is, what they're finding is that lower levels of lead in a house seems to cause slowness in learning, neurological problems, mostly in minority communities. The proposed solution to this problem is to make the owner sheetrock every single apartment where you have a child 6 years or under. Sheetrock it and be done with the problem. That's at a cost of $10-15,000 per unit. It will cost the City of New York roughly $1.5 billion to do it just in the housing they own. Private property owners once again have to shoulder a societal burden simply because they own the property and can't pick it up and move out of the city.

The list goes on and on. Take window guards. There is an ex-Marine who came back from the Vietnam War and bought a building with his brother. A child falls out of an apartment on the first floor that was occupied by his grandparents, there was no window guard. The city brought this property owner up on criminal charges, "criminal negligence" for not knowing that this child's grandparents were away. If he was convicted, and we got him off with a settlement of a lot of money, he would have lost his military pension, he would have literally lost everything that he had gained by serving in the military, defending this country in Vietnam. So you have this situation where the people that we should be embracing, literally the backbone of the City of New York, the small property owner, are being treated like second-class citizens, as if they had no opportunity to pick up and leave this city. And yet when you really look at the true solution to the problems of the city, these people are the solution, they are at the trenches.

Another example, Red Robinson owned a building he was given when the guy he worked for died. He was left a string of buildings on 149th Street, right across the street from an elementary school. A drug dealer broke into the building, actually broke into the basement in the back where a lot of paint used to be stored, lit the paint on fire and drove all the legitimate tenants out of the building. Drug dealers then moved in, and had the audacity and the intelligence to call up the housing department and say "my landlord isn't supplying me with heat and hot water; I don't even have a toilet seat on my toilet". After HPD sent out inspectors, Judge Louis Freedman threw Red Robinson in jail for not providing heat and hot water to drug dealers and squatters who had burned out his building. Ultimately these thugs went up through the roof and burned out the other buildings all down the block. If you go there now you can see the little holes in the bricked-up buildings through which they deal drugs. Then you talk to the people, we went up there and interviewed people who lived in the neighborhood, people who now live elsewhere and come back every day to just to hang out on the stoop or that block. And they say it was a lot better when Red ran this building; it wasn't perfect but there were people on that block. And now when the kids come out of that elementary school, what do they see? They see burned out shells, they see drug dealers dealing drugs by the school, and the bottom line is that one man who could have prevented that from happening, Red Robinson, was thrown in jail for not providing hot water to drug dealers and squatters. That's the way this city and this state treat the people that are footing the bill.

The stories go on and on about property owners simply being unable to do what they're in business to do, which is to provide a service, collect payment for that service, pay their taxes, pay their water and sewer bills and hopefully buy the building next door, and then the next one and the next one. But there's no opportunity, there's lost opportunity in terms of what every single immigrant group that has come to New York seeks. Buying a rundown building, using their sweat and their tears to fix that building up--that's gone. And if that's gone for good, then this city is gone for good.

HL: John, you present a very compelling argument--one I've heard before, and needless to say, I agree with you. But where do you mobilize, or how do you mobilize, the political will to deal with this issue when one out of every seven New York residents lives in a rent controlled or rent stabilized apartment, when you have 250,000 *in rem* units, a startling number since that makes New York City government the largest property owner in this town. Where do you find the politicians, or I should say the grassroots movement, to change the conditions that we have. You may recall that State Senator Bruno, I guess it was the year before last, introduced a luxury decontrol bill in the Senate, and I think the threshold point for decontrol is $120,000,

JG: $100,000

HL: $100,000, and he couldn't get anywhere with it.

JG: It's going to pass this year through the Senate.

HL: Through the Senate, but the Assembly is not going to touch it, you can be sure of that. The question is how do you move the system from what is clearly an economic abomination to one where you provide rewards to the very people that you described, and change the system so that we once again come to respect private property and can expand the housing base where indeed, there is a pent up demand for private housing?

JG: Well, remarkably I see the seeds of it happening. How do you make this private housing market grow? Do it very simply, break it down to the lowest common denominator. Identify property owners throughout the City of New York who own property within specific districts, and you mobilize them and provide them with the back-up, the arguments, the numbers, the facts. And you energize them to become political "hit squads," if you will. Legislators respond to pressure. If they get property owners complaining about a specific issue, they will react. It's been done, they even got Jerry Nadler to come out in favor of property tax reform for small property owners. He sponsored that bill and it passed. And the governor signed it. But what you really have to do is to break down the issue into something that can't be denied. We're producing a half hour documentary precisely on this issue, on New York, the history of New York and why it was built up, why it became the greatest city in the world, and where we are now and what we are doing to preserve that title.

It all comes down to opportunity; doesn't matter if you're African-American, Hispanic, Caribbean, Chinese, Russian, Polish, my mother made me mention Norwegian--she's Norwegian. It doesn't matter, if you own property in New York, you are a second class citizen, you go to Housing Court and you're dead meat. I was quoted in the *New York Times* in an article about a Legal Aid Society spokesmen who sued, saying that every tenant in Housing Court should be represented by legal counsel, and my quote was "well, I do believe that people deserve legal counsel when they're in a court of law, but you don't really need it in Housing Court because you have Housing Court judges who are already tenant advocates."

HL: You've got proponents --

JG: That's right, that morning, the day after the *Times* quote, I got a call from Bruce Gould, who was at that time head of the Housing Court Judges Association, and I thought he was going to yell at me for being so flippant. I could tell he almost had tears in his eyes and he was thanking me, he said: "John I want to thank you as someone who has finally publicly acknowledged the role that we play in Housing Court." I was dumbfounded, I thought he was being a wise ass, I thought he was being sarcastic. And when I hung up the phone I realized he was dead serious. So how do we break this down? You've got to elect public officials who are sensitive to property owners. We've got to get property owners to become active on community boards and in local clubs, whether it's Republican or Democratic, it doesn't matter. We've got to get property owners who are community activists, plain and simple. And it can't be the one issue--we're here because we want to get rid of rent control. It's got to be because we want better schools, we want more cops on the street, we want fire protection.

The answer to all of those things that everybody in this city wants

is a stronger tax base. How do you get a stronger tax base? Put more
people with privately-owned property on the tax rolls. It's plain and
simple, that's the only way you can accomplish the goal. By focusing
on that, by coming full circle, beyond so-called selfish issues, you may
find a solution. If you're a landlord with rent control and all you really
want is to collect more rent, milk the building, and skip out, that's not
what we're trying to defend. The bottom line is that property owners
simply want to be treated with fairness like any restaurant owner or any
other small business person in the City of New York. You know, if I
were in the business of selling turkeys, turkey dinners, and somebody
walked into my restaurant, and night after night ate that turkey dinner
and didn't pay for it and got off scot free, I'm not going to stay in
business very long. But that's what happens everyday in Housing
Court, where owners can not collect their rent for six, seven, eight, or
nine months. We're talking money that adds up to a total overall fuel
bill or total property and liability insurance premium for a year, these
are huge dollars. And ultimately when a judge decides, o.k. we're
going to total it up, and it's ten thousand dollars, we're going to give
a five thousand dollar rebate to the tenant because there should have
been repairs done, even though the tenant wouldn't let the owner into
the apartment. And that tenant says: I've got to come up with five
grand; forget it. They're out in the middle of the night. So the owner
is out ten grand. That's the game that's being played every single day
in Housing Court. There are 350,000 non-payment and holdover actions
brought every single year in the City of New York in Housing Court,
350,000. A lot of lawyers are making big money down there. And a
lot of owners are losing a lot of money.

Commentary: ER

    When John Gilbert was first offered his current job as head of the
Rent Stabilization Association, his friends urged him not to accept.
They assured him that most city landlords were greedy millionaires,
who pretended to be poor whenever rent guidelines were being set in
Albany. There was no future representing such a disreputable group.
    Now, after ten years on the job, Mr. Gilbert appreciates the power
of pro-tenant propaganda to sway even intelligent individuals--such as
his friends. In *Unreal Estate*, Mr. Gilbert has documented the plight of

small property owners in New York City. Most of the landlords he represents face a huge gap between revenues and operating costs. All too often it is their salaries from outside jobs that help them meet the gap. They are not rich: more than 60% own only one building. If they fall behind on their taxes, the city takes over their building.

The inability to recoup costs is largely the result of rent control.

Rent control was originally part of the federal price controls imposed during World War II. Such regulations made sense in wartime, when the supply of new housing was restricted. In those circumstances, market forces will result in higher rents and profits to landlords, but no new construction.

But New York City maintained--and even substantially extended--rent regulations after federal controls were lifted in 1947. By way of justification, city officials claimed that an apartment vacancy rate of less than five percent constituted an "emergency". In fact, the rent controls themselves, by increasing housing demand and throttling housing supply, created the problem.

The original Rent Control Law exempted new construction from regulation. During the 1950s and early 1960s, apartment construction in New York City boomed, averaging 38,000 units annually. However a 1969 law imposed rent stabilization, a mild form of rent control, on properties built before that year. In 1974 the Emergency Tenant Protection Act ended vacancy decontrol and imposed rent stabilization retroactively on all apartments built between 1947 and 1974. The effect was devastating; the number of new apartments completed plunged from 21,394 in 1975 to 8,886 in 1980.

Although rent controlled apartments house a disproportionate share of poor households (24.1%), a significant number are occupied by people making more than $30,000 per year (in 1987 dollars). Many are elderly; the median age of 68 reflects the fact that units typically remain controlled only if the same tenant has been an occupant since 1970 or earlier.

Rent control also has a powerful--and perverse--impact on the income distribution:

Characteristics of Households
by Rent Control Status

	Regulated		
	Cont- rolled	Post-War Stabilized	Decon- trolled
Total Units (000s)	155	273	268
Percent (%)	8.2%	14.5%	14.2%
Median Income	$10,817	$25,761	$19,276
% With Incomes			
Above $30,000	15.0%	43.0%	28.1%
% Living in Poverty	24.1%	10.9%	19.5%
Median Gross Rent	$300	$494	$447
Rent to income ratio	31.4%	25.6%	29.9%
Median Age of Head	68	47	39

Source: U.S. Census Bureau tabulations of the
1987 New York City Housing and Vacancy Survey.

Occupants of post-war stabilized apartments, on the other hand, are, financially, among the best off of all apartment dwellers. The roll call of regulated apartment dwellers reads like a *Who's Who* of New York's political and cultural elite. It includes Lauren Hutton, James Levine, Alistair Cooke, singer Carly Simon, several city council members, and Ed Koch.

Affluent Manhattanites are the big winners. An analysis by Arthur D. Little found that the wealthiest 230,000 households citywide received $500 million in rent control benefits, or $2,175 per household. More than half (52%) live in Manhattan. In contrast, lower income households received benefits worth $110 million, or $515 per household. The higher income occupants of rent regulated housing therefore enjoy benefits 4.5-times greater than those received by lower income renters in the same stock.

To make things worse, occupants of unregulated apartments (mainly in the outer boroughs) are forced to assume the $100 million in real estate taxes that would have been collected if regulated high-rent apartment houses were allowed to charge market rents. In effect, the 1.7 million families not covered by rent control or rent stabilization subsidize the 1.1 million families that are.

Luxury decontrol would be the logical first step in removing these inequities.

When rent regulations force owners to abandon buildings, all New York State residents incur a financial loss. The Department of Housing Preservation and Development will spend $270 million in FY1994 managing buildings acquired *in rem*, through property tax foreclosure. (City-owned housing includes about 30,000 occupied residential and commercial units in apartment buildings, 1,400 occupied one- and two-family homes, and 23,000 vacant houses.) In addition, the State Division of Housing and Community renewal spends $50 million administering the system for the city.

When one factors in the hidden costs, and loss of revenue that occurs when buildings are taken off the tax rolls, the tax cost of city rent regulations, rises to between $1 and $2 billion annually.

But small property owners are the forgotten victims. Most of them invest in real estate to provide shelter for their families as well as a modicum of future financial security. It is a search for the American dream. Municipal bureaucrats, and perverse regulations, have turned it into a nightmare.

4 Interview: Joseph Holland

HL: Let's talk about this whole question of where welfare reform fits into the general state budgetary picture.

JH: Social Service account for about $20 billion of the state's $156 billion budget (in 1994, approximately $24 billion of the state's $63 billion budget,) or more than one third. The biggest problem, of course, is Medicaid, and the biggest problem in Medicaid is long-term health care. We try to peck away at many of the other items, to deliver services more efficiently and cut costs, but long-term health care--essentially nursing home care--is 65% of the problem. The best way to finance long-term care is through private insurance. We must encourage people to buy private long term care insurance at a young age so that when they need such care, their insurance will kick in and cover their costs for three years. After that, the state will defray their nursing home costs. Under this plan there will be no need to spend down assets or hide money.

Unfortunately, we haven't been very successful in getting young people to do this. We were just brainstorming this issue here last week, and we looked into the possibility of talking to insurance companies about a rider on life insurance. Young people do buy life insurance. They may not buy comprehensive policies, but they do buy life insurance. And if we can encourage insurance companies to put in a long-term health care rider, then we could enable people to buy long-term care insurance at a very young age, costing them little money, and a the same time assist the state in solving a major budget problem.

HL: Structuring such an incentive, of course, is the great difficulty. Is there any kind of tax incentive that's possible?

JH: We talked about that, but nothing really has been done. There have been a number of bills or suggestions but nothing has been done to date.

HL: Ed and I were chatting with Ed Reinfurt a little while ago about managed care, and the extent to which managed care experiments have actually worked out quite well. Why not try to introduce some kind of managed care reform proposal for the state?

JH: Managed care is excellent. We have a proposal that's supposed to kick in over a five year period. It has a projected savings of 5 or 8 percent, which is not a lot, but it is a start. It also has an advantage to the client in that the client really returns to a family physician situation, where the physician knows your name and your medical history. So we think that it's a great idea and it's moving in the right direction. People are beginning to believe in it, including the City of New York, where it is really very difficult to get these policies implemented.

HL: One of the questions that was also raised is the extraordinary variation county by county, of long-term care facilities, and the cost of these facilities. Has there been any examination of differences that exist and why some counties have much lower cost per patient care than others?

JH: Some of it reflects regional factors--for example, the prevalence of unionized nursing home workers in some areas. In the city, they're all union workers and they negotiate labor agreements.

ER: But among the rural counties in the northern tier, there's tremendous variation in per capita Medicaid spending. I thought it might just be the location of nursing homes. As Joe said, nursing homes are the biggest single item in the Medicaid budget. So if you have two nursing homes in one county, and none next door, you will have a large difference in per capita Medicaid spending.

HL: But the dramatic difference between Monroe and Onondaga cannot be accounted for on that basis.

ER: When you consider the money that's spend on nursing homes, it could be a significant factor.

JH: Sometimes upstate counties have to send their elderly people out of town, to counties that have nursing homes, so their expense may be even more. You also have to be careful when you talk about Monroe county, because it has a history of controlling health care costs through community rating and other reforms that were implemented jointly with Kodak and other private companies 10 or 15 years ago. So they have a more active cost control program, than, say, the Syracuse area. The Syracuse area, for example, has a geriatric community center with is state-of-the-art, an awesome facility, but it's really high cost. And there is also a very established, non-profit proprietary hospital system right in the Syracuse area. So there are two totally different themes running through Syracuse and Rochester. Even President Clinton's people are using Rochester as a model. So you can use Rochester and Monroe County as examples, but realize that they may be unique situations that cannot be replicated elsewhere.

We were at the Public Welfare Association meeting last week, and some people said that the profit margin in these nursing homes is 30 percent. Whether that's true or not I don't know.

ER: That's not counting the cost of the Medicaid subsidy, is it?

JH: There's a very active debate about that question. There was a press conference yesterday about nursing homes, saying they're losing money on Medicaid, and then the Department of Health saying they're making money on Medicaid and everything else. So New York's Medicaid rates are the highest in the country, and they're higher than Medicare. Our Medicaid reimbursement rates are more expensive, and we cover more people under Medicaid than any other state.

But there is also the question of the legitimacy of our Medicaid rates, and how they relate to cost. Many nursing homes claim they lose money on Medicaid patients and make up the loss on private patients. As a result, private patient charges are pretty high very high, it depends on the region.

HL: Let's look at the other side of the equation, not simply the long-term care but the daily care of poor people. Is there any way to introduce a voucher plan where you say to a poor person, "here's a book, use the vouchers in the book, and when you've used them, that's the end." I mean, why can't a cap be placed on Medicaid for those outside of long-term care?

JH: Politically, the City of New York won't allow us to do that, the Assembly won't allow us to do that. Though we have recommended some caps, and even passed some bills, but we're not going to get beyond that.

HL: There's no understanding or appreciation of the need for a cap in the Assembly. You're saying the Democratic side just won't accept the need for strict cost control?

JH: I don't know if that's totally the problem. There's something like $13 billion being spent on Medicaid services in the City of New York. It's a big part of their economy, and legislators don't want to cut anything, even though they know that it creates a lot of dependency and problems there. The problem with giving poor people a voucher of, say, $10,000 to live on, is that more often than not such persons will manage their money right, and will end up in an emergency situation in the hospital. There has always been that Medicaid safety net. Hospitals have an ethical responsibility to treat people and they can't turn indigent patients away.

HL: I understand that. The problem, however, is the 17 percent per year increase in Medicaid. You reach a point where you drive out all other spending in the state. I mean, all you have to do is extrapolate that growth rate. I'm simply trying to think though the reforms that are needed to engage in sensible cost containment.

JH: Your voucher scheme could only be sued for medical care. It wouldn't be something they could sell to someone else for cash. The voucher program sounds great and it would work probably until December when you ran out of vouchers. What happens when a Medicaid person walks into a hospital and says I need medical treatment. Hospitals have an ethical responsibility by federal and state law to treat that person and do charity care for which they only get reimbursed 60 percent. So you have to change that. It's both a behavioral change and an entitlement change.

I think you also have to consider the fact that we have an incredible underground economy in which all kinds of Medicaid benefits can be "sold" for cash. There are doctors that are willing to do fraudulent things. They will give you $10 for your voucher so that they can cash it, and not treat you. So I think a voucher plan would create a lot of problems. You'd have to find ways to control the kinds of abuses that are already part of Medicaid fraud.

HL: What drives the tax structure in this state to an extraordinary degree is the assumptions that are made about Medicaid. If you start with the assumption that roughly 20, more like 40 percent of the budget is going to be in Medicaid, and you're going to increase it at the rate of roughly 17 percent a year, then you are led to the inevitable conclusion that your tax rate is going to have to go up correspondingly. There's really no way to control your taxes. If such a significant portion of your budget is going up at a rate roughly five times the rate of inflation, what do you do? You are left with the inevitable conclusion that you've got to raise the taxes at least a billion dollars a year, if not two billion dollars. And if you start extrapolating into the future, as I've suggested, then you reach a point by the year 2000 where the tax increase would have to be on the order of four billion dollars a year, just to meet the increase in Medicaid expenses. So unless you attack this problem, and start looking at cost containment, you have a state that is simply bankrupt. There's no other way to control it. I don't mean to give you a lugubrious scenario, and maybe there is some way for intervention, but what I am suggesting is that the intervention has to occur now. I'm not preaching, but I am looking for answers. I'm looking at some of your proposals.

JH: So are we all. You tie in cost controls with the Medicaid takeover now.

HL: But then you also have the state co-opting local taxes, so that's the trade-off. County Executives are now saying "what are we giving up? Are we giving up more than what we're actually getting?"

JH: And they're going to come in at a later date and say "Can you raise my sales tax by 1%, 'cause I can't make it any other way?"

HL: Exactly, so now you have a force that is driving up local taxes as well.

ER: Is it a complete takeover, or just a takeover of the annual increase in Medicaid?

JH: No, it's a complete takeover of the locality share, the county share.

ER: Is that different from the Governor's original proposal?

JH: No, he proposed a complete takeover by the year 2000.

HL: It's moving incrementally.

JH: Yes, we would do the same thing. Our program would do the same thing. Except we wouldn't take the local taxes.

HL: What is the chance of passing the Medicaid takeover bill?

JH: There is a lot of pressure to do it.

ER: I thought the Republicans would be against something like that because it would hurt the upstate group vis-a-vis New York City. The city has more to gain from a Medicaid takeover than rural counties.

JH: The figures show that the city does better by it, that's true. But the upstate counties are pushing us too. If they get the cost containment, the upstate counties will benefit from this plan too. And there are more Republican County Executives than Democrats.

If we could get the federal government to take over long-term care we would be sitting in the driver's seat too. Any maybe the federal government--if it did take it over--could say to New York, "Hey, you have to make some cuts here or we're not going to do this." Tough sell though.

HL: It's a tough sell but maybe that's the answer, with the federal government saying we'll absorb this, but we expect you to engage in some kind of cost control Can we chat for a minute Joe, about your perception of the budget, where you think it's going, what's going to happen this year? Are we moving toward some reasonable conclusion of this budget process? Where do you think it's going to be a few years from now? If there is a two billion dollar increase in taxes, the consequence for businesses in this state is likely to be what it has been for the last two years, a hemorrhage in job loss.

JH: He's talking about a $3.7 billion increase in taxes.

HL: That's because of the new taxes and because the last year of the tax cut was put on hold indefinitely.

JH: And the corporate tax, that's right.

HL: The surtax remains on the board.

JH: I believe, that from an economic standpoint, we are improving, and that our economy is getting better, and that three or four years down the road we will have the money available to do what we need to do. But right now it's going to cost money.

ER: But if the economy is getting better, it's not because of any initiatives on the state level.

JH: That's correct. We're chasing business out of here. I come from a border community. If you look at Rockland County, or Orange County, you'll see that we chased all our gas stations away because our gas prices were so high because of taxes. Now we're going to raise our cigarette prices to 60 cents a pack, and instead of bringing four truckloads of illegal cigarettes into the City of New York, it'll be ten. There's no question about that in my mind. But I don't think we're going to change that until we change this Governor, and I told the school board members Saturday that this man has a very liberal philosophy, and his commissioners do also, and until we change him and his commissioners we're not going to be able to start on the road back to conservative government.

HL: More clearly, economic growth and tax reduction are going to have to be the two factors that come together. I think even if there is some improvement, and as Ed is pointing out, it's not as significant as the improvement that is likely to occur in some other places in the country. New York is in a competitive position with a lot of other states. The question becomes: Why be in New York if there really is no opportunity for you here? We just heard a lecture on the value of small businesses, and the extent to which they are creating jobs, which we all know. But it's invariably the small businesses that take the hit when it comes to taxes. They're the people that are likely to leave.

JH: It's fun discussing it, and its interesting. Unless we have the federal government take over long-term care the state's budget problems will persist. Such a takeover wouldn't solve everything, but it would get us off the hook.

ER: Well, the tax incentives for the purchase of private long-term care insurance will only bear fruit in the distant future, when those people get old and become eligible for long-term care. But in the meantime you still have the Medicaid problem, unaddressed. I thin managed care, as you mentioned, is something that will reduce costs by maybe five percent, at best. This think isn't going to be fully phased-in for a number of years anyway. What intrigues me in Medicaid is that you have a lot of people in nursing homes who are certainly not poor. Medicaid is a program for poor people, but you have a lot of people hiding assets. You know, they say they are spending down, but they're really comparatively well-to-do people who can easily afford the nursing homes. There's a whole gaggle of lawyers in New York State that make a living out of making you appear poor in order to qualify for Medicaid. And because lawyers are such a powerful lobby, they're probably calling the shots, and would squelch any effort to stop this scam.

JH: We've worked on this for three or four years now. What you come up against is that for every scheme we shut down, three more pop up, and a lot of it is apparently allowed by federal Medicaid law. There's leeway there. When they did the Medicare Catastrophic Act, they also changed the Medicaid provisions, but when they repealed it, they didn't repeal the Medicaid provisions. So they tried in 1989 to get at that problem somewhat, but there's still enough leeway to allow people to get around the income and asset limits. We've done a number of things to crack down. Last year there was actually a trust provision in the Medicaid bill to crack down on the trust loophole. It was heresy five years ago to even talk about that issue. But that was debated at the conference, and implemented postactively, not retroactively. You know there are a lot of things that happened there. One of the schemes was to transfer assets a little at a time, therefore getting around the penalty period. We shut that down in New York State. But as I said, until you decide who is going to pay for long-term care, this problem is not going to go away. Our Congress and the President have said all along that Medicaid is going to pay for long-term care.

HL: The problem is that the eligibility requirement suggests that anyone who owns a home can't get Medicaid. Take a widow who wants to transfer that home to her child because it's her only asset. Instead of giving it to her child after she leaves this world, she's going to give it to the child while she is alive. But now she has no assets; now she becomes a ward of the state.

JH: You're right. The federal government says 30 months is the transfer period. (This has since changed) So no one is liable for nursing home expenses in this country if they dispose of their assets before they need the care. One of the things New York State has done is to participate in the Robert Wood Johnson Foundation project for long-term care insurance. I don't know the exact date, but we should be seeing some financial benefit in the next few years, it's being pushed over month by month.

HL: What is the Robert Wood Johnson project?

JH: It's a public project to get people to buy insurance. I think there is a whole slew of people out there who are up to transferring their assets and would prefer to buy a policy for a few years even if they're now 60 or 65, and even if it's going to cost them thousands of dollars. To them, in their financial situation, that would be a nice option. We get calls all the time from people who want to buy these policies. I think the savings from such insurance would occur far more quickly than people realize.

ER: You mean these are elderly people who want to purchase long-term care policies?

JH: Elderly people are calling us all the time, but we have to see what the cost is and then make the decision.

HL: Well, obviously the cost might be prohibitively high for most people, if you're buying insurance and you're 60.

JH: But the exposure to the insurance company is capped after three years, then Medicaid picks it up. The actuary showed that it's going to work out, most people don't want to go to a nursing home. What you're doing, again, is another question of entitlement. One aspect is people want to give wealth away, they want to pass wealth to their family and protect themselves against larger care costs. Did we solve it all?

HL: Well, you raised the right questions.

ER: What about workfare? Is there any initiative along those lines in New York? I know Clinton is making noises there.

JH: Workfare is only implemented in two counties. We're trying to get it in the City of New York. Workfare should work. It should chase people off the welfare rolls and put them to work. It works in Westchester County. The City of New York, and the legislators from the City of New York are against it. It's not a Republican or Democratic issues, it's the City of New York versus the rest of the state.

HL: But it is ostensibly a Democratic/Republican issue. You're just being kind by making it a bipartisan issue.

Commentary: HL

I recently met a 23 year old woman in Rochester who has three children, all born out of wedlock. This woman dropped out of high school at 16 and had her first illegitimate child at 17. When her first child was three years old, a welfare agent told her she must seek employment or her benefits would be cut. She dealt with that demand by having her second child. Three years later she had her third child. Now she receives $24,000 of direct AFDC payments; in addition she receives a housing allowance, Medicaid, food stamps, child care, and travel expenses to and from the clinic. Her total benefits package is $38,000. My accountant notes that in order to receive $38,000 of benefits, one must earn $51,000.

My eldest daughter is about the same age as the woman from Rochester. After graduating from Vassar College Phi Beta Kappa, she sought employment with a magazine in New York City. Her starting salary was $19,000 and she paid local, state and federal taxes on that sum. A portion of her taxes will assuredly be employed to address welfare assistance in New York.

What, I ask, is the message being delivered to young people by this profile in contrasts? Is hard work rewarded or is immorality rewarded? At what point does the state wake up and dismantle a welfare bureaucracy that daily engages young people in a Faustian deal that provides immediate benefits and long term despair?

Few people in the state government are more knowledgeable about this subject than Senator Joe Holland. Senator Holland understands the dilemma my scenario poses and he is equally sensitive to the cost of long term health care, which is 65 percent of the Medicaid burden. But acceptable solutions, he notes, are not on the horizon. HMO's, or managed care, will reduce expenses by an estimated 5 to 8 percent. Private insurance schemes established in anticipation of long-term care can offset the cost of nursing homes. And changing the Medicaid reimbursement formula so that physicians can receive more than the allotted $10 a visit rate, and hospitals can charge less than the $150 a visit rate, also seems warranted. But whether these reforms will have a dramatic effect on the growth of Medicaid expenditures is problematical.

The real solution--placing a spending cap on Medicaid calibrated to what the state can afford--isn't in the offing because members of the New York State Assembly consider this proposal politically unacceptable. After all, as Holland notes, the $13 billion spent on Medicaid services in New York City alone represents a large part of the economy and many jobs. Even if a cap were established, there wouldn't be a penalty on those who didn't manage their health care vouchers effectively because hospitals are obliged to assist even those patients who don't have the means to pay for health care service.

Considering the rise in welfare and Medicaid expenditures as a function of the state budget, the day is coming when a $2 to $3 billion increase in taxes each year will be necessary to meet the anticipated increase in these two items. Perhaps that explains why the state government has proposed a takeover of the Medicaid system by localities, albeit any takeover in effect represents a trade-off of local sales taxes for Medicaid relief. Nor does this address the spiralling increase in costs; all it does is shift the burden of paying for it. The corollary suggestion of enlisting federal government support is more of the same--passing the buck to another level of government.

Yet, and this is the real issue, the increase in taxes brought about by welfare and Medicaid costs are driving private sector jobs and business out of the state at an alarming rate. Unless these budget items are brought under control, the anticipated expenditures will have to be paid by putting the state into ever greater debt, which threatens to crowd out private capital even further. Tax reduction and economic growth can point the state in the appropriate direction, but these factors are proscribed by an inability to reduce the state budget, specifically welfare and Medicaid costs.

Only by restoring a sense of personal responsibility can the state assure a reduction in its expenses--a goal that is often contradicted by bureaucrats who sustain themselves with additional clients. Here in undiluted form is a system devouring itself. If welfare were considered temporary or emergency assistance, expenses could be controlled. Similarly, if people in their 40's and 50's purchased long-term care policies, the burden on the state when they are in their mid-60s would diminish. But these conditions are based on the belief that personal responsibility transcends an expansive state authority, and that prudence and pragmatism should be encouraged in order to reduce the size and expense of government and that "free-ridership" can destroy the incentive to provide for oneself and family. All of these notions are currently out of favor.

5 Interview: Stephen Kagann

HL: The movement in legislatures and city councils seem to be toward ever higher taxes because they cannot see a way to develop a consensus for retrenchment. If this is true, then how do you move political agencies in a direction that will allow the tax burden to be either frozen or rolled back, so that once again we create a more congenial environment for investment, and not crowd out private capital. Obviously, this is the $64,000 question--a little different from what you're concerned with, but maybe we can start the conversation in that way.

SK: Well, I can speak of my hopes. The people in Albany tell me that there is no turning back, that the present high tax/high spending system is here to stay. They tell me they appreciate my work, but I should not be naive. I should understand how the system works.

I joined Andrew Stein because I want to make these issues part of the political debate. And if this next mayoral election is decided on economic issues relative to the city's general population, perhaps it might be viewed as a mandate for serious change.

At the level of the state legislature, one of the things that bothers me, is that a lot of the things that damage the city are created or approved in Albany. The New York City delegation must be voting for them.

HL: Oh, without question, in the assembly it's predominantly Liberal Democrats.

SK: Whether it's the hotel tax, the parking surcharges, or all the New York City income tax surcharges--the state legislators from New York City who are going to be endorsed by the New York Times for re-election have voted against the interests of New York City, and nobody calls them to account for the damage they do. I'm hoping that there will be enough political change so that if not this year, then maybe in the future, New Yorkers will begin to realize what their state legislators cavalierly do to them.

HL: But is there a real understanding of that? I mean, part of the problem is to raise the level of consciousness among voters in New York City. When they are told, "Well, you're not going to get your $200 million grant from the state government," they are appalled, but in fact they wouldn't need the $200 million if they didn't have the mandates and the taxes imposed on them by the state government. But they don't understand that. Now the problem is: How do you develop that level of understanding? The political sophistication among New Yorkers is not so well-developed that this problem is well understood.

SK: I've spent six years in Rochester, and I believe that the people in Rochester are much more sophisticated when it comes to elections than the people in New York City. Maybe because we've had 30 years of city government expansion, the elections are never fought in New York City on the same self-interest of the voter. Instead, the arguments are over the demands of government, government programs for special interests, and so on. Real self-interest would dictate that people begin to consider what expanding government means for their own jobs, their careers, their futures, and their place in New York City. I hope that my own work will begin to create some greater consciousness. I feel like Don Quixote.

HL: I've long felt like Don Quixote, so join the crowd. But let me ask you, suppose Andy Stein is elected Mayor--an unlikely scenario, but let's just say that happens--or let's just say for the sake of argument a Herb London or someone else is elected governor of New York, what would you do in order to deal with the problems that we are now confronting on the tax and job landscape?

SK: As a minimum, the Mayor must consider fundamental managerial change. By my estimate, city employment is probably 50% larger than it ought to be compared to other cities. That suggests that good management, something I don't remember in New York City, could bring down the cost of government substantially. That's the first thing. Second, there must be privatization of many city functions. It is within the Mayor's power to begin to do some of that sort of thing. My experience in the private sector tells me that quality of service could improve even as we cut cost.

HL: Could a mayor be re-elected if you have 300,000 city workers who routinely vote for a Democratic candidate? Could an Andy Stein be re-elected if he eliminated 20% of that labor force?

SK: I think he could. If you can change people's minds about the nature of city government. If you can change the belief that there is a correlation between government spending and government services, by reducing the size of government and delivering better services than ever before. The rest of the world is doing it, the corporate world, universities, other governments are doing it--why not here? I think it would work politically. I really believe that city workers--whose jobs are so boring--would welcome an environment of improvement and quality of service delivery; job satisfaction will improve. The union leaders may not like it, but city workers will be happier.

HL: You're also aware of the fact that in the city we have more than a million people on welfare. Many of the jobs that are created in this city are an extension of the welfare program, and so what you have are 300,000 city workers, of whom maybe 100,000 or more are potential welfare recipients. They're not going to find jobs in the private sector. In fact, every time I go into the municipal building, I find people who sit around eating cupcakes and potato chips all day, and they call this a job.

I had the experience very recently of going up to, I think, the 31st floor where WNYC is located to do a television program. Well, there's not an elevator that goes directly to the 31st floor, so I had to get out on the 28th floor. I get out at the 28th floor, and I couldn't find the elevator to the 31st, so I go into an office, I don't know what office it is, and I said, "Excuse me, could you direct me to the elevator to the 31st floor?" This person said, "Get on line!" It's a long line in the room. All I want is the elevator--they're on line for papers, or a license to get married, or I don't know what--all I wanted was just directions to the elevator. Just tell me where the elevator is, but he acted just like a bureaucrat, just like what you might expect.

SK: Right. I have a research assistant who is very good at ferreting out information. Her frustration is that when she calls people in Washington or in the private sector, she always gets cooperation. But when she calls somebody in the New York City bureaucracy, they ask, "Well, what do you want it for?" "Maybe you should get her a note from your supervisor to my supervisor that you should have this information." This kind of attitude is encrusted, and it's bad. Good management can change it. I would hope that a different kind of administration would choose as its managers people who really know how to manage change, rather than lawyers, campaign aides and those with political connections.

HL: Well, the hope may be realized. I now feel somewhat inspired by Andy Stein because you're on his payroll, and the fact that he would appoint you clearly suggests that maybe he is serious about fundamental changes in New York.

SK: I know it's a longshot, but if he were to be elected on a platform of downsizing government, and cutting taxes, and re-creating New York City as the business capital of the country, I think we could regain some of our lost status. It may happen. It would be interesting if Stein won the primary. Then you'd have two candidates who are talking about the need for an economic turnaround in the city, and getting government off the backs of those in the private sector who create jobs and income.

HL: Yet neither would do something as radical but obviously necessary as going head-to-head with the proponents of rent control.

SK: Certainly not during an election campaign.

HL: Exactly, and I don't even know if they would do it subsequently, because there wouldn't be a mandate--

SK: Well, rent control is one of the many problems. My analyses show that we're losing our private economy in a major way. If you cut taxes and regulations, you can generate improvement.

HL: Let's say you were to eliminate some of the nuisance taxes in New York. Some fairly obvious ones come to mind: the commercial rent tax, for example.

SK: Every mayor since Wagner has said he would eliminate it, but none of them has ever done it.

HL: That's largely because there is no constituency for it. It's very hard to build a constituency for it. But at the state level, the elimination of the state capital gains tax would do an awful lot for the economy. What would happen if we started to introduce those kinds of tax reforms?

SK: Suppose we have a program of tax reduction, particularly those taxes that do the most damage. The commercial rent tax is one, the income tax is another, the double and triple taxation of business income is yet a third. I think we can reverse the economic decline. But there has to be a believable plan, one that decision makers can feel confident about. Otherwise they won't sign long-term leases, and they will not commit to a New York location. Business will continue to move jobs across the river. New York could reverse the lost jobs. Over time, in three or four years, you might be able to get net revenue gain to the city from having a stronger economic base.

ER: Have you ever examined the impact of regulations that don't involve money transferred from business to the government, but impose a cost on business? They are not in the budget, but they're an enormous factor in New York.

SK: I haven't really examined it in any analytical way. But I hear from small business owners that city fines are backbreaking. They feel the city is harassing them. The city is a revenue machine.

HL: By the permit industries--

SK: The city subjects businesses to numerous regulations and forces them to buy permits just to stay in business. Look in the Green Book, the city directory of government agencies. It has about eighty pages of agencies requiring permits and approvals to do just about anything. Some of the most bizarre things that you can imagine.

ER: I've heard that the regulations are even more burdensome than taxes in many ways because they take a lot of time to comply with.

SK: They take time, they reduce private sector productivity, and raise costs to the business. These costs are passed on to consumers, or the firm closes or leaves. It is no accident that the cost of doing business and the cost of living is higher in New York than just about any other location.

ER: There is a common misperception that the problems in New York City are greater than in other cities, which in some sense justifies all this spending. Studies show that we are *not* the poorest city, we do *not* have the worst crime rate, homelessness, etc. But most people who just read the newspaper think that we have unique problems in New York, and have no choice except to spend more money, and raise more taxes. Cuomo has made a career out of this, a very successful one. The question is: how do you change that perception?

SK: There's a wall of denial about why the city is failing. They'll say it's the national recession, it's Bush/Reagan policy, it's crack and AIDS...they've got a whole list of excuses. Everything except the role of New York State and New York City in our decline. These are excuses for failure. It's a convenient tool, I've heard politicians say, "Well, don't ever expect New York to be low-cost town." Well, why not? Is there some law of nature that says this must be? At a minimum, we should benefit from economies of scale.

HL: The big problem, of course, is the municipal unions in New York and the unwillingness of New York politicians to go to war with them. That's what it would require. I mean, after all, the sanitation workers in New York City have a mandated four-hour work day. Obviously it's going to be expensive to collect garbage in New York. When you've already written into law the fact that sanitation workers don't have to work longer than four hours a day. I don't know how you would tackle that one unless you were willing to redraft the contract, go to war with the legislators who were responsible for it, and that requires an enormous amount of political will.

SK: It has to be done.

HL: Of course it has to be done, but there has to be some sort of catalyst for it...

ER: I have a way to do it: welfare reform. Now, seriously, you don't have to be a genius to be a garbage collector. Let's put the one million recipients on the trucks, train them, and pay them a wage slightly below the minimum wage. So that if something comes up in the private sector they'd take it.

SK: I am not an expert on welfare reform. But there is a strong correlation between the loss of private-sector jobs and the rise in the number of welfare recipients. It is a two-way relationship.

There are two possible scenarios. One is a fiscal breakdown. The other is that someone is elected on a platform for change. Change seems unlikely because at the moment they've balanced the budget. They balance the budget on the back of the economy, leading to more companies and families moving out of town. And that may mean more problems a few years from now.

People are asking "why are city revenues holding up if job losses are 100,000 a year, 200,000 a year?" This is happening because most of the people losing their jobs now are at the lower end of the scale. They do not pay much in taxes. But that is why the welfare rolls are rising.

And so people call this a fiscal crisis because people look upon the government and the economy as independent of each other. Was there a fiscal crisis in the 1970s? It was an economic crisis of enormous proportions where 16% of all working New Yorkers lost their jobs, even as national employment increased by 18%. And to call it a fiscal crisis is the equivalent of saying, "The Great Depression was a time when the bureaucrats in Washington had trouble balancing their budget." It's the human cost that's important.

HL: I think you're absolutely right, but the reason why it could be described in that way is because people were aware of the Ponzi Scheme that was organized around bonds, that the city issued bonds to pay off bonds, and kept doing that, and finally it reached a point where the banks said, "I'm sorry, we're not going to accept these bonds any longer," In that sense, it was a fiscal crisis. But you're absolutely right, I mean, that was a ruse. That was simply one explanation for what was a very obvious, larger economic crisis.

SK: At the moment there's no fiscal crisis for most people. The New York press has not noticed. There has not been a discussion of the role of government and economic losses in the *New York Times* since the 1960s. Fiscal problems are treated as a separate issue.

HL: So they are selling bonds, and from their point, they're still generating revenue, and the New York City bond rating is still investment grade at the moment, so they don't see a crisis. And you see that's the problem. That's the point.

SK: The rating agencies did not downgrade New York City's bond rating until after the crisis hit in the 1970s. They did not recognize the problem until it was too late.

ER: Compared to the present situation, 1975 is seen as purely a fiscal crisis because now we have social problems that are supposedly intractable and require government attention--homelessness, AIDS, crack, and all the rest--which we didn't have in '75.

SK: There were other things that they talked about at the time.

ER: They didn't seem to be as terminal as what we're confronted with today.

SK: Government employment and spending in the 1970s continued to grow rapidly five years into the economic collapse. The economy began to collapse in '69, and it wasn't until the fiscal crisis in '74, '75, that they noticed "We're flying, and the rest of the economy is collapsing." By the way, that's almost exactly what's happening now. The Dinkins administration may have had to pull back a little bit in terms of government spending, but the private sector is collapsing so fast that, on a relative basis, government spending is still rising.

ER: The revenue estimates must have been better this time around.

SK: When?

ER: In the last year.

SK: Perhaps, but two years ago they were forecasting good times ahead.

ER: Okay, well, in '75, I was part of the Beame/Lindsay team, you know, and I know how they made their revenue forecasts. They started out with how much money they wanted to spend, and they worked backwards into a revenue forecast.

SK: Until the new fiscal crisis in October 1990, that did not change. But now they have no choice. They are trying to be more realistic in their revenue estimates.

HL: Let me come back, Steve, to the question that you raised before about taking on the unions. Take, for example, privatization in the New York school system where the American Federation of Teachers is very well entrenched. How could you introduce a kind of voucher plan, which would make sense in a place like New York, where you have a fairly expensive parochial school system with a tuition of about $2000, and a $2000 voucher would allow many poor Blacks and Hispanics to send their kids to the Catholic school system, probably give them a better education, revive the Catholic school system, and I think eliminate so many of the marginal public schools in New York. How could you do something like that in a place like New York where the AFT is so well ensconced?

SK: I do not have a lot of knowledge in this area.

HL: Then let's forget that, talk about private garbage collection in New York. Rudy Giuliani says he fears Mafia control. Frankly, I don't even care, because at least you could get some efficiency. But suppose you had competitive bidding, and you had private garbage collection competing, not necessarily replacing, but competing with the public garbage collectors in New York. What would the sanitation union do? They would be out on strike the following day. And let's just say for the sake of argument, you were to eliminate all those people who service a bottleneck in the subway system, giving out tokens for your money, and do what I have proposed and that is, give out tokens to every bodega, every McDonald's, let them buy tokens for $1.15 or $1.20 and sell them for $1.25. Eliminate all these people, they don't serve any purpose anyway. The next day, everyone who's employed by the MTA would be out on strike, every transportation worker in New York would be out on strike.

SK: Well, let's go back to Lindsay. By the way, I voted for Lindsay, I supported him, and I figure I'm doing penance now. The day that he was inaugurated they began the subway strike. I'll never forget his speech about how we're not going to give into the power brokers. The union leaders broke his back. The city is owned and operated by special interests. At some point somebody has got to stand up and say, "All right, we're going to take the heat."

HL: Well, you've got a Philadelphia mayor who's willing to do it. I just don't know whether an Andy Stein or a Giuliani would be willing to do that. I mean, maybe you're right, maybe Andy Stein has that requisite spine, that backbone, to stand up the unions and take it, but I just don't see much evidence of this anywhere in the New York system, even Koch.

SK: I can't speak for Stein.

HL: Obviously you can't, but I think there are a lot of people who realize what has to be done. But it's a question of whether you can muster the political will to do it, whether you can find a constituency that would be willing to back you up. This guy in Philadelphia impresses me a great deal, Rendell, because I think he did force the unions to back down.

ER: He had no choice. I mean, their problem was a lot worse than ours.

HL: Well, I don't know about that. I think the problem might be described as comparable, but we have not been able to elect a leader like that, who in the very first quarter of his first year went to war.

SK: There are over three million people in New York City who get up and go to work every day, most of whom have no part of the government. Many are at risk of losing their jobs. They see their standard of living falling. But they're not an organized group. They may be the biggest part of the population. Nobody speaks for them. There may be a way of creating a collective consciousness of working people, of educating them to what their interests are. That may be what Rendell is doing in Philadelphia. And I have a feeling in New York it would be the same. But since they're not organized, the politicians don't respond to them.

ER: The classic public choice conundrum. You have a few special interest groups for whom it makes sense to fight for what they want, and three million ordinary folks. Whatever they get is divided by three million, so who cares?

HL: You know, that's a very good point. That's the problem with rent control. Not that people don't understand that they're paying a fee for rent-controlled apartments in New York, but that you can't organize them. When I used to say to people, "You're paying for the privilege of Carly Simon, Woody Allen, and Mia Farrow to live in rent-controlled apartments," they say, "Well, everyone else is..." You can't get a rouse out of anyone in this town.

SK: That's true. That is what I would change, like Don Quixote.

HL: And thank God there are Don Quixotes like you.

SK: Look at it on the national level. President Bush had 90% popularity ratings a year and a half ago, two years ago. What's different? One, there's no war, and second, national employment levels are down by 1.5%. In New York City, if you take the private sector as I define it, the non-government supported private sector, we're down almost 15%. Nearly 400,000 people lost their jobs since April of '89. And this is not an issue!

HL: I thought 500,000 since June of 1990, statewide.

SK: That's a reasonable number, because almost 400,000 have occurred right here in the city.

ER: These numbers are incredible!

SK: And the people in government are so busy saying, "We're not responsible, Bush did it to us, Reagan did it to us, the national economy did it to us," and the press parrots it. *The New York Times*, which I mention because it set the agenda for the politicians, repeats these arguments. Although anybody that you talk to out on the street says,

"It's really disgusting what's happening to the city, it's declining, this is costing more, my job is at risk, my store is going out of business because there are no more customers." Everybody's aware that something's wrong. But no one wants to take responsibility. What I'm hoping to do is create a sense of responsibility. We're doing it to ourselves.

HL: Well, I think the Manhattan Institute is very good at publicizing your ideas. Your piece in the *Wall Street Journal* unquestionably generated a lot of interest, and the piece in the *City Journal* has been distributed widely; I've got about seven copies that people have sent me!

SK: Historically this kind of story has never created a political consciousness in New York. People are concerned with maintaining their jobs and their standard of living, supporting their families. They have little interest in what the mayor or governor is up to because they have been fooled or are cynical.

HL: Have you looked at this, Steve, on an industry basis? The garment industry or financial service centers?

SK: Unless you're in the health business or the social welfare business, you're not doing well.

HL: But are some more adversely affected than others? Would financial services be any worse off than, say, the garment center?

SK: The garment industry is probably worse off. Financial services are what everyone hoped would save the city. The securities industry...

HL: Which was OK until '87.

SK: Every wise commentator said that when Wall Street returned to profitability they would start hiring, and the money would come back to the city. But what are they doing now?

HL: Every back office operation is in New Jersey, they're not here.

SK: I hear that Salomon Brothers has a policy that any job that doesn't have to be in New York leaves New York. So, even though the industry is doing well, they're moving the jobs out of the city.

ER: But isn't employment in that industry up?

SK: No, the rate of decline is attenuating, but the jobs are still dribbling out of the city month by month. The companies are moving people out. Even as they do some additional hiring, net on balance, the city is losing national industry jobs. And other financial industries, such as insurance, are quietly slipping out of town. Nobody noticed that insurance employment has gone down dramatically over the last decade. And the banking industry, of course, is contracting. So the financial services sector is no great boon to the city, even though it does well.

The worst industry of course is retailing. Retail sales are falling faster than everything else. And who works in retail shops for the most part? Mostly, they're young workers, marginal workers, people who haven't established themselves yet. The Hispanics are suffering because they are disproportionately represented in retailing, and also disproportionately represented in manufacturing. To me, of course, the worst is manufacturing.

We are told "the immigrants will save us". That's nonsense. Immigrants traditionally went into manufacturing, and there are no manufacturing jobs here anymore. This isn't the 1940s or 1950s, where you had a million manufacturing jobs.

ER: On the other hand, the immigrants are keeping the cost of living down for a lot of the people who stay in New York. The Korean grocery stores--I couldn't survive without them, my lunch would be $15 instead of $4. As an economist, I have to look at the general equilibrium of this thing, and it's almost like the North American Free Trade Agreement. We're going to lose some jobs, but we're also going to import a lot of cheap stuff from Mexico that wasn't available to us, and that will more than offset that income loss.

SK: That benefits the city in the sense of improving consumer welfare. Your welfare as a consumer improves because you get better products at lower prices.

HL: You get a lot of non-union workers, Koreans, who are working the garment industry who cannot be employed by the people on 34th Street, but you can find them in Long Island City of even downtown in New York, working in what is the modern version of a sweatshop, and producing pretty good products at a reasonable cost. That's the sort of thing you buy at a flea market. But you can find that everywhere. And I think there's a market for it, and I think Ed is making a good point. In the general economic climate, those people do offset some of the high living costs of New York.

SK: Going back to specific areas of the economy, the one that upsets me, in addition to manufacturing, is the loss of corporate headquarters. I remember when New York was home to nearly one-third of the largest American companies. Corporations that had no business being in New York still wanted their headquarters to be here. No other city would do. We were home to utilities from Pennsylvania and oil companies from Texas. You could build a career in any industry, right here in Manhattan.

There were different levels of opportunity. If you graduated from high school, maybe you sought a white collar job. Your father may have been a factory worker, but the school system turned out a supply of capable people to work in these offices. So it was a system that worked. Now the back office jobs have moved out. The level of opportunity is a small fraction of what it used to be. That thing that made New York exciting was that many of the best people from the rest of the country came to New York. They came because they had ambition, they lusted for money, they lusted for power. People don't do this anymore. This is a real loss. Everything is closing in. The school system doesn't provide qualified workers. Graduates can't find jobs. They leave and the tax base weakens.

ER: I think these intangibles are very important, we've lost our cache as the Big Apple being the place to be if you want to make it. It's technological obsolescence to some extent; the communications revolution has enabled other cities to compete with New York.

SK: The communications revolution is just an excuse for the city's failure to keep business here. It allows them to leave if they want to. The voracious appetite of government drives them out. London and Tokyo are two cases in point. They also have the communications revolution, but nobody wants to leave town.

ER: And the rents in Tokyo are probably higher than they are in New York.

SK: In fact, they tell me that the Japanese government would like some dispersal from Tokyo. They can't get people to leave. They have a real problem, there are too many people, too much concentration, too much overcrowding, and they can't get people to leave.

ER: And they have an excellent transportation infrastructure, they can get to Tokyo if they had to from other parts of the country.

SK: Yes, they don't have to be there.

ER: What about crime, do you think crime is as important an issue in location as taxes? Do you deal with it in your model?

SK: In the new study that we released two weeks ago about the loss of corporate headquarters, we demonstrate a clear relationship between the crime rate and the loss of jobs. This is interesting because it confirms opinion surveys. Price Waterhouse conducted a survey of 300 executives in six New York industries, and found that the second most important reason companies consider leaving the city (after costs) is city-wide security. Crime makes a difference. It's statistically significant. We call the crime rate "variable quality of life," because it's probably related to homelessness, panhandling, and everything else that's going on.

The apologists for failure like to say this is the cultural capital of America. We have the opera, museums, and so forth. All of which is true, but in the survey of the 300 executives, the least important factor in the location decision was the city's cultural and educational attractions. This is ironic because the major cultural institutions were built by the business leaders who came to New York after the Civil War.

ER: Another economic factor is the value of real estate. In recent years many individuals have lost wealth in New York, probably more so than in any other city in the country, because of the collapse of real estate prices. A lot of people who may have regarded the city as a good investment, as well as a nice place to live, are stuck here now. Is it possible to quantify that? Would that be an interesting thing to look at?

SK: I don't know. I haven't really looked at it, except as it relates to my work on taxes. The real estate market was a bubble that had to burst. The city hitched its revenue wagon to a speculative boom. When the bubble burst, tax rates and assessment kept rising--just like the 1970s. One result of rising costs was a further decline in real estate values. This is another way people have been hurt by government.

ER: I remember trying to explain how the 1986 tax code was really going to be good for real estate because it would bring interest rates down, and offset the loss of all those tax shelters that were driving the prices up.

SK: In the early 1970s I really wanted to buy a brownstone in Greenwich Village. You could buy one for about $150,000, but I couldn't afford it. Seven years later of course, these brownstones were worth over a million. Who was paying these prices? Doctors, and other high income people. The certain losses offset other taxable income. While the federal tax code increased the demand for properties, the 1986 tax code changes helped to kick the props from under the market.

Commentary: ER

"To suggest municipal government is responsible for the loss of 400,000 jobs in a recession is nonsense. People say, "What about all those jobs you lost? Well, we didn't lose them!" - David Dinkins (*Crain's New York Business*, 7/19/93)

"We feel it's the fault of the recession." - First Deputy Mayor Norman Steisel, on the cause of rising welfare rolls (*NY Post*, 9/18/92)

The national recession ended in March 1991. Since then, employment has risen slowly in the most of the nation. New York City, however, remains in an economic freefall. Since 1989, private sector payrolls have fallen by 11.4%, to levels not seen since the last prolonged downturn, 1969 to 1977. As late as March 1994 the city's unemployment rate was 10.3%, versus 6.8% for the nation.

But economic reality has yet to penetrate New York City politicians.

David Dinkins still blames the city's slump on Washington, Albany, and the national business cycle.

Steve Kagann, on the other hand, shows the wound to be self-inflicted: a large and growing disparity between the Big Apple's tax burden as compared to that in the rest of the nation. In New York City, state and local taxes consume 17.8% of gross city product (GCP, the total value of all goods and services produced in the city). In the rest of the nation, the state and local tax burden is only 9.5% of GCP. More importantly, the tax gap between New York and the rest of the country--7.6 per cent of GCP--is three times wider than it was forty years ago.

The taxes support a municipal budget that exceeds that of any other large city in the nation, either per capita or as a percentage of income. New York City also devotes a far larger fraction of its budget to social spending and hospitals. Mean while, items that could benefit business are given relatively short shrift. In FY1991, for example, the city spent a total of $74 million of city, state, and federal funds on economic development programs, out of a total expense budget of $28 billion and a capital budget of $4 billion. Education also accounts for a far smaller share of New York City's budget than it does in most large cities.

At one time city officials could believe, with some justification, that local taxes had little impact on the city's economy. Taxes represented a small fraction of the cost of doing business here, they were deductible against federal personal income and corporate taxes. Moreover, a Manhattan location was indispensable for many large U.S. corporations. Taxes mattered little when national or even international prestige was at stake.

But the Big Apple has lost much of its shine. During the past three decades, New York City lost two-thirds of its Fortune 500 headquarters. Today, only three of the top 50 industrial companies are headquartered in the city, and they have pruned payrolls by 20% in the past decade. The health care industry, financed in large part by government funds, is now the city's largest employer, eclipsing corporate headquarters, banking, real estate, and publishing.

The tax trend is well known to people in New York City government. So is the exodus of companies from New York. What is missing is any acknowledgment of cause and effect. In research done for the city Comptroller, Kagann gets right to the point. Several factor prompt businesses to leave, including technological innovation (e.g., the fax machine), the lowering of real transportation costs, and various quality of life issues such as the crime rate.

But taxes are the key. According to Steve Kagann's statistical analysis, each $100 million in additional city taxes leads to the loss of 11,400 private sector jobs citywide. He estimates that the tax hike enacted at the start of Dinkins Administration was responsible for nearly two-thirds of all jobs lost during 1990-92 (209,000 out of 349,000 private sector jobs).

In other words, the administration turned a mild correction into a rout.

Kagann estimates that every private sector job that is lost costs the city $6,800 in tax revenues, including the secondary impact on property taxes and other areas. And this figure ignores the cost of welfare, which increases in lock step with unemployment.

The good news, according to Kagann, is that the process is reversible. Broad tax cuts will attract new businesses and stimulate expansion of existing ones. Unfortunately, New York City officials wait until firms are halfway out the door before offering them tax breaks, hence the wheeling and dealing with AT&T, Morgan Stanley, Mobil, and other large corporations.

The city's targeting is all wrong. Most jobs created in New York City in the past two decades have been in small or mid-sized companies. Unfortunately, these firms lack the political and economic means to cut their own deals. Thus, tax cuts for large inefficient companies have meant higher taxes for smaller companies that represent the economic future.

With more than 25 separate city taxes on the books, policy makers might wonder where to start cutting. Kagann's research provides some answers. The commercial rent tax, for example, is a *de facto* tax on jobs that escalates with every new lease. Since its inception in 1963, nearly every New York City mayor has acknowledged its destructiveness, but none has acted to abolish, or even phase out, the tax. The unincorporated business tax also gets low marks for taxing income that is already subject to the city's personal income taxes. Many business owners respond to double taxation by moving out of the city, taking with them their earnings and their spending.

Taxes aren't everything, however. A skilled labor force may be the single most important prerequisite for economic growth. Yet city schools are failing. A recent study shows that 31% of New York City public school students do not graduate. Those who do often lack the skills needed to handle entry level positions in upcoming employment fields such as health care.

Equally alarming is the diminished attachment to work or job search among New York City residents. This is best measured by the labor force participation rate--the percent of the population working or looking for work. In 1992, the participation rate in New York City was 56.3%, significantly below the 66.0% rate for the nation. More New Yorkers would be working if incentives were the same as in the rest of the nation.

Popular explanations of the low participation rate include a large underground economy in which people work "off the books", and generous welfare benefits that facilitate unemployment.

Steve Kagann would undoubtedly add taxes.

State and Local Tax Burden

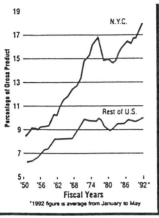

SOURCE: N.Y.C. Comptroller's Annual Reports. Office of N.Y.S. Deputy
Comptroller for the City of N.Y. Government Finances.
Bureau of the Census

Total Employment (Seasonally Adjusted)

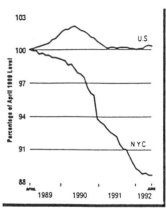

SOURCE: U.S. Bureau of Labor Statistics. N.Y.S. Department of Labor

**Growth in Government Employment
Relative to Private Employment**

SOURCE. N.Y.S. Department of Labor

6 Interview: Edward Koch

HL: In our conversation with Henry Stern, we talked about the problems associated with the budget. He made the point right out of James Buchanan's thesis on public choice philosophy, that the direction of the budget is toward increasing its size. He said when you were mayor, you would say to the City Council "We cannot increase the size of this budget, we can't have new jobs." And he said even though he was sympathetic, he still asked for more jobs in the Parks Department. How do you develop a consensus, or can you develop a consensus, for retrenchment?

EK: It's not hard to do. The fact that David Dinkins is doing it suggests as much. When you take inflation into consideration, it means that any budget a commissioner gets this year must be more than last year, just to keep the same services. The city has not been doing that; therefore, even if the commissioner has exactly the same budget as last year, he must reduce services. But I think that even under the current mayor, and I don't think he's so terrific in these areas, the government has reduced expenses. How do you get commissioners to do it? Well, if they don't believe you, they're not going to do it. But I think city commissioners today believe the mayor when he tells them that there is a budget deficit. And when he gives them targets, they understand that they must be met. The budget director has to say to commissioners, we want you to come in with savings in your agency of two percent, four percent, or whatever it happens to be, and lay out for us whatever it is that you are going to eliminate in order to make that saving.

You generally give commissioners a target which is greater than what you actually need because there are some agencies where you can't get that reduction, for example, Human Resources Administration (HRA), since 75 percent of that agency's money is not city money.

Every dollar that you eliminate from HRA means you're eliminating three dollars that belong to somebody else, which is tough stuff. Nevertheless, you must take cuts there as well. So you give them across-the-board targets, some agencies lessen targets because some things are mandatory and cannot be reduced. What happens, in my experience, always was that in the beginning, until they know that you're not kidding around, they will offer up cuts for things that absolutely can't be cut, thinking that you know these can't be cut and therefore you won't cut them. But the budget director isn't that stupid nor is the mayor that stupid. So what happens is you put them on notice. Listen, I would say, these are ridiculous cuts; if you don't think you can do the job then we will tell you where to cut. That's one thing that a commissioner absolutely doesn't want--cuts imposed upon him. Therefore once they get the message they will come in with the least adverse effect on their agencies and with the targeted cuts. If there's a problem, there can be a discussion or an opportunity to appeal. Appeals go first to the budget director, who never relents, and then to the mayor. On occasion that's fine. I think some of the cuts that the city government took last year are ridiculous. To achieve what they told us is a 500 million dollar surplus, they cut out the rat control program and the school repair program. That's not achieving a surplus; ultimately they'll have to put the money back in anyway.

HL: Let me ask the question in a slightly different way because what you've just described is very much related to executive leadership, and clearly you provided it, particularly after the crisis that you had to face in 1977, the year you became mayor, but the 1975 fiscal crisis was a different matter.

EK: There were three fiscal crises: The one in 1975, and in '77 and '78. The crisis in 1975 was basically solved by Governor Hugh Carey with legislation. But the problem wasn't solved, so that when I came in, I was faced with it. He was never one to give me credit for resolving it because he would like to be perceived as the *eminence gris* to the mayor of the City of New York. As a result, there were all these fights between Felix Rohatyn and myself. I always would say "Look Felix, if you want to be mayor, run. You can't be mayor while I'm mayor." Felix now tries to eliminate from history what happened in '77 and '78 as an economic crisis but he can't because he sent out a letter on January 20th of 1978 to the members of the Municipal Assistance board, it goes something like this: hold on to your hats, you ain't seen nothing yet; the crisis that we are coming into now is far worse than the crisis of 1975. He was right. So what they thought they had solved in '75 was a short term financial crisis, caused by federal seasonal loans, because nobody would lend us money pending our taxes being collected. All you needed to do, he thought, was to deal with a cash flow problem. But it was actually a structural problem that you had to deal with.

In '78 New York City got the federal guarantees that allowed us to restructure debt, and allowed us to go back into the bond market by insuring the pension funds against loss. The city needed a capital budget, which it didn't have when I came in. When I came in the capital budget was $349 million, of which half was city-derived tax levy and the balance, not much of a balance, was state and federal money. When I left, the capital budget was $5 billion. We dealt with that crisis, and it wasn't easy, and it required pain. The problem that I see with David Dinkins is he does not provide the charismatic leadership required in a crisis. The City of New York, the mayor, the governor, even the president, have to accept economic cycles. A recession or a depression is typical, that's the nature of our society. What you have to provide during this period of crisis is a sense that somebody is in charge, that somebody will lead you across the desert and across the Red Sea. David Dinkins can't provide that, there's nobody that sees him in that way.

HL: I think the point that you're making is an excellent one but during this period when there's less money available due in large part to the cyclical nature of the economy, it becomes more difficult to raise resources, more difficult to pay bills. Is there ever a mandate from the people for the kind of fiscal reform that you talk about or is it necessary to educate your constituents after you've been elected?

EK: There are very few people who in public life have the courage to do what is right.

HL: So that if you run for office you really can't tell the people what is necessary.

EK: Oh I tried. I think I did, I think I had the courage to do what had to be done. In fact when I ran I said things are terrible, things are going to get worse, we're going to be cutting the budget, we don't have enough money to do everything. Whereas David Dinkins was telling everyone how much more money he's going to spend just like Clinton is doing now. But I, because I'd been there, I knew. You may remember that when the stock market fell in 1987 I took immediate action, I put a job freeze on, I reduced expenditures, although the governor and City Comptroller Jay Goldin criticized me. They said: he's panicking, he's doing this much too quickly, it's not necessary. I had to hear their critical words, but I was very proud of what I did and I was right and they were wrong. Maybe that's why you need limitations on office, because there comes a time when you have to say, so if I don't get elected so what, there's life after death.

HL: You've demonstrated that.

EK: I've demonstrated that. I always knew that. I mean I wasn't going to disappear, I'm enjoying my life, this is my third career, filled with joy and no anxiety.

HL: What a wonderful position to be in. Let me switch gears slightly and move from the city to the state level. Here is Cuomo, he's facing a fiscal crisis of his own, a large part of it he blames on George Bush, but that I suppose is partisan politics.

EK: He has to be asked the following: How can you blame the fiscal crisis of New York on George Bush, when we are, I think, the forty-ninth state in terms of bond ratings, almost the lowest. That means that 48 other governors apparently were able to do better than you. So how can you blame the feds? And with all of our resources New York State's budget is the third largest in the country: First, the federal budget, second, California and third, the State of New York, and fourth, the City of New York , I mean what's going on? I proposed to Governor Cuomo that he examine all of our social programs because they provide Cadillac service compared with the other 49 states, and I said, "We are number one in providing all of these services why not be number five? Then 45 other states would be doing worse, and only four other states would be doing better. If we don't have the money we can't be number one." And he laughed. He also got angry, and this was on a radio program, so he said: "What is Koch suggesting, that we

have the number five baseball team?"
    In the private sector, if you can't afford to be number one in terms
of quality players, you may go to number five. Not everybody is
number one. While we can't afford it, we insist on being number one.
I gave this proposal to the Manhattan Institute and I think, they
concluded that the state would save $4 billion on an annual basis if they
did what I suggested in just the most important agencies, and the city
would save $2 billion. And it's not as difficult as zero-based budgeting,
which is too hard to do, because you have to start fresh every year. I'm
not saying that. I'm just saying we're number one, let's ease down to
number five. It's not hard to do, if you have the courage to do it.

HL: You anticipated the next question I was going to ask about the
kind of reforms that you indicated when Change-NY talked about
bringing us down to the fifth or sixth level in welfare assistance. You
say it takes courage, and these decisions are largely unilateral; the
governor of New York has the authority to make them. But how would
you develop a political consensus? Let's assume you were running for
office. Put yourself in my position.

EK: I'll tell you how you do it, Perot almost did it. If he had the
courage to stay in the race and run candidates for every congressional
seat and every senate seat, then even though he would never have won
this time around he would have established a force that would be
ongoing. Now he's just an airhead, an empty suit. I never established
an independent party, but ironically, maybe I should have. I don't think
I could have, frankly.

HL: It would have been hard in New York.

EK: Yes, very hard. But Cuomo can, and the reason is that Cuomo is
really a political animal. I'm saying that with some affection. He has
a party following; I never had a party following. I had a following that
was in the public, but that is very ephemeral support, because they're
with you but please don't ask them to come out in the rain. So I never
had what he has, which is party hierarchal people who would follow
him even if it meant they were making a break with county leaders. He
would offer them jobs, I wouldn't do that. You know he had the
Liberal Party, he had a whole apparatus, and he could have started an
independent party. And he's a great orator. I don't know anyone who

has his ability to make speeches, to persuade. He's unique in that area. But he has not used it to do the hard things, only to do the soft things, namely to help himself.

I did not use patronage for appointing judges, I did not use patronage for people who have policy-making positions. I irritated everybody. It's the strangest thing, I never got credit for what I consider to be a revolution in politics: For eliminating political appointments when it came to judges, that's unheard of. The best illustration is: I knew that my government had to have an Italian as one of the commissioners, so I went out of my way to get one and that's not unreasonable. It wasn't part of the gorgeous mosaic where I had quotas, but you can't have a government that doesn't have a black, an Italian, a Jew, an hispanic, whatever it happens to be in some high position. There has to be representation. I don't consider that unreasonable. Dinkins, by contrast, runs the government on the basis of quotas, but he's honest about it; he says he is for racial quotas. He is for racial quotas in personnel appointments; he's for racial quotas in contracts for the city. I'm not, I never was and I took so much heat for standing firm on that issue. But Cuomo doesn't hesitate to use patronage. You have to distinguish between what are called discretionary jobs and civil service jobs and see whether he fills them in a patronage way. The fact that it is not a civil service job doesn't mean that you have to fill it in a patronage way, which means that you are rewarding people who have served you or you are delegating the responsibility of filling the job to someone else in politics. You need the best people in managerial positions who represent you, not civil service philosophy or politicians. Otherwise the government comes to a stand-off. Provisionals, meaning the civil service at the top level are often the best people in government.

HL: Tell me where you think New York City and New York State are going, if you had to make some sort of prognosis.

EK: I'm afraid for New York City, and I'll tell you what I'm afraid about. I'd like to think we'll come out of the darkness, I think there's a sense of foreboding; we've already seen the middle class flight. Just the other day I was talking with a lawyer who lives on the west side in the 90's, very wealthy, he has two children. He said I just sent my daughter away to a prep school. I didn't really want to do that. She's out of town now, but it isn't safe for her to walk around the streets;

she's thirteen years old, and when she wants to visit her friends, I would say "How are you going to get there?" She would say, "I'm going to take a taxi daddy." "How are you going to get back?" "Well, I'll find a taxi." "I'm not going to let you walk around the street, looking for a taxi to get back here," he said. "You know the streets are filled with criminals, alcoholics, drug addicts, mentally disturbed people, I can't let my kids walk around that way, I'm afraid for them." Well, he's rich, and he's sending his kids to prep school, but the middle-class people don't have that money. But they can send their kids to a good school in the nearby suburbs. They will find a suburb that has a good school and move. They'll save a lot of money, lots of city taxes, and that is what's happening.

The City of New York, I think has lost 400,000 jobs since David Dinkins came in--I don't blame him for the economy--but I must say that the employers who are leaving don't have confidence that he can lead the city through this crisis and create an environment that will keep people here. That's what I worry about. This city is a unique city, it's a city that has a minority of whites. In most cities that have a minority of whites, that minority almost becomes extinguished because they leave in ever-larger numbers, the so-called "tipping point." Birmingham, for example, has very few whites left in it. I was there the other day, it's a black city. Nothing wrong with a black city except the center of the city where all the stores are located is vacant. You go to Detroit, that's a city that will never come back. I worry about it, I don't think that will happen to New York City because the diversity is here, 25% black, 25% hispanic, 6 or 8 percent Asian, 42% white, whatever the figures are. So I am hopeful that we will not see happen to us, what has happened to other cities. It will take a new mayor who will create the confidence necessary to keep people here.

HL: At the state level job loss is at 570,000 over the last four years, and that's a big number. Taxes have gone up dramatically. A young man going into business today, starting a small software company, for example, is going to look at Texas, Florida, Nevada, California, and say, "I don't know, should I be in business in New York and pay the bills for the rather expensive welfare program and other programs in New York State?".

EK: Everybody talks about high tech, it's baloney, everybody talks about enterprise zones, it has nothing to do with anything. What counts is confidence; nobody in his right mind is going to go to a crime infested area just because the taxes are lower. Where are the employees going to come from? You think that your middle class employees are going to a crime infested enterprise zone? They're not. So I say to myself, why are they so hung up on those enterprise zones? We have enterprise zones in New York City; I don't know that they've created any new jobs. The city has created many new jobs by putting in a lot of money in particular projects, but that's not what we're talking about. The private sector requires assurance. Freedom from violence and an educated workforce are absolute necessities and the private sector at the moment doesn't believe that those two ingredients are here to make an investment in New York. Now I haven't checked the departure rate but I don't think there is yet a mad rush out of here, but I worry about it.

HL: The net departure rate in 1991 according to the Moving Authority of New York is 49,000, the largest since the Great Depression. And the state departure rate in the decade of the eighties, is about 1.4 million. In the first two years of the 1990's were up to about 120,000 out of New York State, so the numbers are impressive. I don't know if that could be described as a hemorrhage. But the numbers are impressive.

EK: I worry about it.

Commentary: HL

If governmental leadership is measured by one's ability to convince the public to embrace unpopular ideas because they are necessary to sustain the body politic, former Mayor Ed Koch clearly qualifies as a leader. It is apparent from his remarks that New York City is in his blood; he embodies the best of its spirit. Whether Mayor Koch's solutions to current problems are appropriate is another matter.

While a mayor can impose budget restraints on his commissioners, he must cope with a variety of forces that drive the price of municipal services inevitably higher. Jawboning alone doesn't usually work with city employees as the mayor well knows. It is at the margin where costs can be contained. Despite his best efforts, the New York City budget rose significantly under his stewardship.

It is accurate, I believe, to emphasize charismatic leadership in a

crisis.   Since all governments are subject to economic cycles, the
manner in which downturns are dealt with is critical.   Surely there are
few people who have the courage to do what is right as Mr. Koch
indicates, but what is right isn't easy to determine.   History is written
by the winners who do what turns out to be successful, or who have
good fortune smile on them.

I emphatically agree that New York State can lower the expense for
welfare without adversely affecting poor people.   (Is it really a sign of
New York's prominence that we are number one in welfare payments?)
Since welfare and Medicaid payments constitute 41 percent of the state
budget and are rising at the rate of 17 1/2 percent annually, a ten year
extrapolation suggests these items will crowd out all other state
expenditures.   Is the right decision to reduce welfare or to eliminate it,
as Wisconsin Governor Tommy Thompson has done?

It can also be argued that the estimated 36,000 patronage jobs in
New York State go beyond the demands of party allegiance and
personal power.   But eliminating many of those jobs, even those Mayor
Koch calls concessionary jobs, means going to war against one's own
party organization in an effort to reduce the magnitude of the budget.
That, in my judgment, would be the right thing to do, albeit some
would judge it an act of political suicide.   It is worth asking how many
patronage jobs are necessary to sustain a political organization, and then
conclude that any above that number are superfluous.   That calculation
isn't made.

In the long-term, the "confidence factor" is what is critical to city
and state.   When a politician restores confidence that is flagging, almost
any other decision is irrelevant.   A belief that conditions will be better
than they have been is a source of political strength.   President Reagan--
whatever programmatic deficiencies can be found in his administrations-
-did reverse a widespread sense of malaise that developed during the
Carter years.

At the moment, the confidence factor in New York is at its nadir.
Mayor Koch merely approached the tip of the iceberg when he referred
to conditions on the city streets.   Urban areas everywhere in the state
engender fear.   Fear is the overriding New York concern.   Simple
pleasures such as sitting in a park, taking a stroll in the evening, or
reading a newspaper on a commuter train have been transmogrified into
possibly dangerous episodes.   No one, not the rich or privileged, are
insulated from the fear; it surrounds the city as a perpetual haze.

People migrate from New York because they don't want to be a crime statistic. Whether the fear is based on a realistic assessment is less important than that it exists, and exerts an influence as a social catalyst. For any politician today, the confidence factor translates into a modicum of security in the streets, in the schools, and in public conveyances. Without that security, all the tax reforms won't amount to a hill of beans. New Yorkers will not sacrifice their future for a few extra dollars.

As Mayor Koch notes, the reason tax-incentive business "enterprise zones don't work in New York is that they are usually located in marginal neighborhoods where sensible people don't travel unless they must. Saving two percent on an item in an enterprise zone located in a high crime area is not a trade-off most people entertain. Freedom from violence is what New York's constituencies desire and what few politicians can deliver within the constraints of the law and the present interpretation of civil liberties. Hence the conundrum of political life is, how do you engender confidence when crime is on the rise and the practical solutions to it aren't easily found? Like Mayor Koch, I too worry about this.

7 Interview: Dick Netzer

HL: ...Wherever you stand in politics, I believe that there probably is some consensus on what has to be done to improve life in New York State and New York City. But there are great political impediments that prevent people from moving in an appropriate direction.

DN: I don't think there is a consensus. There is a small number of people who believe there is presently too much government. Too much in one of two directions: either through overstaffing, or in the number of different functions performed by the government. New Yorkers generally believe that there are some things that shouldn't be done by government. Most will say that the Department of Education at 110 Livingston Street is full of bureaucrats, and we shouldn't have it. That's true, but 110 Livingston Street looks exactly like every other city agency, and looks like every state agency.

But I don't think that many New Yorkers feel that way. Instead, most believe that, when new problems present themselves, the city government must act, even if it means adding staff, which is exactly what the Koch administration did between 1983 and the end of 1989. There are scandals in foster care, so a new agency is created to supervise the people running foster care. If the supervisory agency doesn't work well, create a new unit to supervise the supervisors. It's fifteen more people here and twenty five there and thirty five here and at the end of five years there are 50,000 more people on staff. I think somebody at the Office of Management and Budget (OMB) in the city could go through that 50,000 expansion, and find a tag line to justify every single one of them. But when it all adds up, it makes no sense.

HL: There are several things that have occurred. Number one, it is widely known, but perhaps not as widely known as I would like, that there are now 540 city employees for every 10,000 in the population.

Detroit, the second highest, has 206 per 10,000 in the population. That's a dramatic difference. Number two, the oppressive tax rate in New York is, I think, fairly evident to New Yorkers. All they have to do is look at their pay stubs. And number three, the departure of people from New York is now reaching a rather alarming rate; 1992 had the highest departure rate since the Depression--49,000 people. Those who leave are obviously not the indigent, not the poor, not those on welfare, as you well know. I think that there is a growing realization that the city and state are in a long-run decline. I have no way of measuring this. Maybe you're right, and only a very small number of residents realize this. But I think that more and more New Yorkers are aware of what is going on, and sense that something is wrong in New York.

DN: I hope so, but I'm somewhat pessimistic, because I think that the majority attitude is a result of decades of conviction that whatever the problem is, more government is the way to go. Thirty years ago city and state governments thought state government could do anything. It started before John Lindsay became mayor, the idea that if there's social problem, hire people, do something.

ER: The context in which that view developed was within an economy that was growing very robustly.

DN: Absolutely.

ER: But the world has changed--

DN: But the one thing that was as true then as it is now, is that many of the problems that the city and state thought they were going to solve by action of some sort or another simply can't be solved by government. They didn't have the slightest idea of what they were doing then. They were just as impotent then as now, although the city and state governments were flush. And what bothers me is that even now lots of ordinary people think somebody should be doing something about a long list of social ills, which are probably insoluble by government. Perhaps government can help by withdrawing. Periodically, there are stories in the *New York Times* and elsewhere about problems with the regulation of taxis and limousines. My view is that the one useful thing the city government can do is to stop regulating the industry at all, safety and insurance requirements aside. Don't deal with regulatory problems by new rules and more staff to enforce more rules. But that's not the advice that comes from civic groups, special interest groups and study commissions: they recommend more government.

HL: Aren't there some visible symbols that had an effect on the population. Aaron Wildavsky wrote this piece that you've probably read, that said if you want to understand what's un-American, look at the Brooklyn-Queens Expressway.

DN: That's right. The first time he said it, he said it at a small gathering in 1976.

HL: And its even more true now, because the BQE construction is still not completed, and here we are in 1992. Aren't there many people, and not just those with a cynical view of government, who are coming to the conclusion that maybe government can't do all the things that we would wish. Maybe it is as powerless as you suggest. Don't those symbols say anything? Don't people come to the realization that government isn't always the answer?

DN: I worry about that, because there does seem to be so much pressure in the other direction: "let's do something about it." I am absolutely convinced that the city would be better off if political decisionmakers in office occasionally said 'no, we can't do that, we don't know how to do it, there's no way we can solve it.' Or, 'it's too bad, but I don't know what to do.' Or maybe 'there's something we're now doing that's causing the trouble.' But that doesn't happen. Unthinking activism is not a universal practice of politicians in democratic societies, or elsewhere in this country. It is much more characteristic of New York than any other place I know.

HL: Well whatever you think of Ronald Reagan, there was a certain degree of humility that he achieved. I remember chatting with the President and if a subject came up where he felt the government couldn't do anything, he'd say, 'I don't want to discuss that issue, we can't do a damn thing about that.' I think that showed an element of humility.

DN: Oh, I think that's true. It's highlighted with his successor, President Bush, who doesn't think that way at all.

HL: Tell me what you think could be done. What would be the three things you would concentrate on in New York State? Forget the city for a moment. What could be done if you were in the position of organizing New York State government?

DN: If you look at what the state does, you'll see that it has some direct responsibility where it actually runs programs, but most of its money goes to local governments. The state runs prisons, the state universities, the mental hospitals and much of the highway system. That ends what the state does. And it doesn't do any of them very well. In each case there are constraints, so you can't say "the commissioner didn't do the right thing", because the commissioner doesn't have the power to do the right thing. People have been saying that for years about the mental hospitals.

HL: We had a conversation with Parks Commissioner Henry Stern in which we got into public choice philosophy. We were talking about public transportation, which in New York State is an allocation system instead of a market pricing system, largely because there are political impediments associated with it. How do you move from this kind of allocational system, where the political impediments are actually quite profound, to a system which from my point of view makes a lot more sense which would be a market pricing system.

DN: I think what is needed is chipping away at old ways of ding business by demonstrating successes in more and more places, and more ways. Each change of them takes a lot of guts. This is true for roads as well as for public transportation. Someone should ask, for example, what form of transportation does the state subsidize most heavily? It is the commuter railroads. They are incredibly heavily subsidized. And what is the consequence of the subsidy? Just look at the payroll on the LIRR, which is far higher than anyplace else.

  I have an anecdote that shows the advantage of market pricing: it concerns LIRR service to the Hamptons. The LIRR has 25 percent of the business, and two private bus lines have the rest. The bus fares are about twice as high, in some cases three times as high as the cheapest fares on the LIRR. But the bus lines get most of the business, despite the fact that the LIRR is heavily subsidized and the bus lines are not.

ER: Could the LIRR be privatized do you think? Is that possible?

DN: Paradoxically, the LIRR and the other commuter railroads
probably could be privatized now, but were forced to become public
charges in the 1960's and 1970's: their physical plant was in terrible
shape and the finances of the parent private railroads were in ruins,
largely as a consequence of decades of destructive federal regulation
and state taxation of the railroad industry. But billions of dollars of
public money has been put into rebuilding the physical plant, so that it
is conceivable to privatize now, rather in the way that Conrail was
privatized after it was reconstructed with federal money between 1976
and 1983, and substantially deregulated.

    There are two real prerequisites to privatization. First, no private
commuter railroad can make it if its main competitor--the use of private
motor vehicles for journeys to and from work--continues to be
massively subsidized, as it is now. Second, there must be a labor
relations regime that makes it possible over time for labor costs to be
reduced to reasonable levels, as has happened with regard to the private
freight railroads since 1976. The subsidies to the commuter railroads
produce a lot of service to thousands of people, but it is clear that
operating subsidies have been mostly swallowed by very high labor
costs, ludicrously high in the case of the LIRR, far above the high labor
costs of the New York City subway system. Moreover, there is still a
lot of the old tradition of families passing these great jobs on from
generation to generation. This is bad enough in the construction trades.
This enterprise should be better.

HL: With government subsidy.

DN: Right. So I think this is an area where there are opportunities for
shrinking the scope of state government.   Another is in higher
education. I support the proposition that has been advanced many
times, that state universities should charge full cost tuition and offer
student aid.
HL: I've been arguing that for a long time. I mean it's wrong to
subsidize upper-middle class students in the state university. Charge
them a real tuition and then provide scholarships.

DN: Right. These numbers have been calculated for the states, too. Perhaps most important, this would change the character of the place.

HL: Oh, without question.

DN: It would probably mean less change in the city university than in the State University system. That's where the change is going to occur. You would get a lot less high cost programming at particular campuses, and some campuses would collapse.

HL: It's no loss. If you come from a family earning a couple of hundred thousand dollars a year, what they do is they give the kid a new car, so they go to the State University of Binghamton. I'm always struck by the number of BMWs I count in the parking lot--not in the faculty parking lot, but the student parking lot. These parents are making a financial judgment, not an academic one. They're saying "Go to this school and we'll give you a gift to go there." So they're not sending their kids to NYU, they're sending them to state university and paying $1950 a year as opposed to the $20,000 they'd spend at NYU.

DN: I certainly think that if the state university did it that way they could increase the number of kids from low-income families. They could increase the number because there aren't many at the state university campuses! The City University has many more lower-income kids.

HL: I don't think City University would be greatly affected at all by this.

DN: Very minor effects. Only a few city institutions would shrink.

HL: Queens College maybe.

DN: Kingsborough Community College is another.

ER: But those kids would probably go to private schools.

DN: They might very well. Nassau Community College might just go out of business. That's a classic point of view where parents say to the kids, go to Nassau Community College for two years, then I'll give you the BMW, then go to Binghamton.

ER: That's a good illustration.

DN: When we turn to the big money that the state provides to cities, it's in the area of health and welfare. These areas are so regulated by the federal government that I think it's hard to say that New York State does it wrong compared to everybody else, because everybody seems to do it so badly.

HL: There were some recent stories that show New York is somewhat worse.

DN: Yes, somewhat worse, but I think it's hard to separate out. On the school aid side, the state has an equalization system, so the issue is not a question of inequitable or equitable treatment in the school districts, the question is the extravagance. The present financing system just produces incredible levels of spending for nothing. Expenditures are much higher in New York than in other states, taking comparable kinds of schools. Districts in other states do just as good a job as New York, in places that have the same socioeconomic characteristics, and cost so much less. The blame must be on the state because the State Education Department has legal, statutory provisions that make no sense at all.

HL: You also understand the political quid pro quo. I mean, Marino signs on to the Cuomo budget largely because of the extraordinary aid given to education in Nassau County. Their per capita student expenditure is now $8500 compared to the $7800 in New York City. And I'm not sure that they're getting $8500 worth of education since the prep school Exeter's tuition rate this year is $9500--not significantly different from what you have in Nassau County.

DN: You know, school districts charge each other for out of district students. The East Hampton High School tuition rate is about $15,000, their average cost per pupil. It is a very small high school with a very good program, so the per pupil costs are very high.

ER: Well, who lives there during the "off season"?

DN: The people whose kids are in school are ordinary people, who work in the service industry, and those who pay the tuition live outside the East Hampton school district. The East Hampton school district includes the most valuable residential property, largely second homes. There are other school districts in the East End of Long Island that have less in the way of estate property to tax, and their tax rates are not particularly low.

HL: I guess a lot of seasonal property out there pays full fare with the property tax even though they don't have any kids there in the winter.

DN: Yes, the East Hampton school district itself has low tax rates despite spending its money like it's going out of style.

ER: I mean it's better than having commercial property because you don't have to give services all year. There's nobody there for most of the year.

DN: The only service that many people get out of the East Hampton school district is an excellent library, which is subsidized very heavily by the school district.

ER: Yes, and the tennis courts as well.

DN: Yes, the use of those facilities. But you know, there are tennis courts everywhere in the place, privately owned.

ER: Can you write a scenario where school choice could catch on in a big way in New York? This notion of giving people vouchers for so much per student, and letting them create a market for schools, private or public.

DN: I would start off by requiring the districts themselves to provide a wide range of alternative schools. But most of the districts are incapable of doing that. The East Harlem school district is probably the only one in the state that does that now. It has been doing so for a long enough time so you'd think it was easy to emulate. It isn't. I don't think it's just the bureaucratic restrictions, I think it's the opposition of the teacher's union.

ER: That's part of it--

HL: But what Ed I think is suggesting is would you create a market for this kind of innovation if you had these vouchers, if you saved $2500 out of the $7800, and said to parents, "You spend the money in a manner that you consider fit."

DN: I would be inclined to offer a wide range of choices. If you offer vouchers, then the district has to either operate a wide range of schools or facilitate opting out. Or it could do both. But a district can no longer have twelve schools that are identical. I'd try to put pressure in both directions. I think you can have something like the British tradition of the schools themselves being able to opt out of the local district. I'd try to have very wide range of choices, to let different things catch on in different parts of the state. You'd end up with lots of schools that are still run by the public school districts. Of course, that is precisely the object of competition: the pressure to change, and innovate, and be alert. But what I worry about is having a system in which there are no public schools left.

HL: Well, that's a legitimate fear, and of course, it's the specter that teacher union president Al Shanker raises all the time when he refers to vouchers that are simply going to decimate the public school system.

DN: I think that's overdrawn. I'm bothered with some of the things Shanker has written. I don't see why he goes up to a certain point and then stops dead. The next logical step is more choice, more vouchers. I think that he makes a stronger case for school choice than anybody else, but then he says, but who's going to make the decision? And he doesn't like the idea of other people making the decision.

HL: Ultimately what Shanker is suffering from is a kind of professional schizophrenia because, after all, he has got this union constituency that he has to appeal to. In private conversations, he's really quite reasonable.

DN: I think the constituency that he's appealing to is the constituency of teachers who are least professional, least concerned. My younger daughter is a critical care nurse, ICU. She very early concluded that the curse was the union, and the union was really against anything that would improve her life, and only did things with great reluctance, and had to be conned into doing things that were advantageous to the most professional among the RNs, like salary differentials related to skill and degree of responsibility. Many hospital nurses are like many teachers, loosely attached to their careers in their early years and, if they do remain working as nurses, eventually are just as happy with jobs that do not entail a lot of responsibility and a lot of emotional stress, like critical care nursing. Salary differentials would not be helpful to that large group of nursing union members, so the union tends to be negative about professional interests and goals, and overly concerned that more individual responsibility on the part of nurses could be tough on some of them. The parallel with the teachers' unions, especially the NEA, is strong.

Commentary: ER

Dick Netzer is a world-class economist. He has written extensively on state and local taxation, including a book considered by many to be the definitive work on the property tax. His intimate knowledge of the subject leads him to conclude that tax cutting alone cannot save New York State.

Netzer's views on tax policy are set forth in a 1986 article tellingly titled "What Should Governors Do When Economists Tell Them That Nothing Works?" It is absurd, he says, for governors to assume that businesses are oblivious to state and local tax costs, but equally absurd for them to believe that "there is usually a big bang for the buck."

Economic theory tells us that, other things being equal, high-tax states will lose businesses and jobs to low-tax states. The problem, according to Netzer, is that the non-tax factors that influence location decisions are never equal. Indeed, the advantages of doing business in a particular location are often overwhelming, "so much so that even extraordinarily high taxes on these activities in one state will not induce moves to another state." [p.22] The tax variable, furthermore, "must be a minor one in location decisions, compared to labor costs, transport costs, market access, access to raw materials, and other similar variables." [p.21]

Perhaps. But couldn't a state's tax and expenditure policies influence the cost of those other factors? Dean Netzer implies as much in the interview. Albany's formula for school district aid, he notes, has pushed per student spending in some politically favored, patronage laden, districts to $15,000 per year, or nearly twice as high as Exeter's $9,500 tuition. State subsidies to the Long Island Railroad have created a payroll that is "off the scale" of anywhere else, and train fares that, "at their cheapest," are three times higher than subsidized bus fares over the same routes. Similarly, barriers to entry erected by New York City for its yellow cabs have pushed fares to stratospheric levels with no commensurate rise in service.

Clearly, high taxes aren't the only anti-business factor in New York's economy. The state's profoundly anti-enterprise climate-the regulatory restrictions, the hostile decisions in the courts, the state's constant meddling in business affairs-are equally significant.

Nowhere in the nation is it so difficult to start a business as in New York State. If you are an unemployed worker and want to drive your own cab, you will have to come up with $120,000 for a taxi medallion. The alternatives - become an employee of the taxi company, or drive an illegal "gypsy cab" - are unacceptable to individuals wishing to better themselves. By contrast, in Washington DC, all you need to drive a taxi is a city license that costs $70.

Want to start a hairdressing salon? First go to cosmetology school and pass the exam. Then you must apply for a state license. Your employees must do the same, even those who just shampoo customers' hair. And when you are finally established, be prepared to contribute to a worker's compensation fund that covers injuries incurred off, as well as on, the job.

But taxes may well be the crucial determinant. Dick Netzer's tax cut skepticism is that of a professional economist scrutinizing evidence persuasive to everyone except professional economists. New York State's economy is was doing badly before 1977; tax rates were excessive relative to those in other states. After the top personal income tax rate was slashed, the state's economy started to outperform the nation. Did the tax cut strengthen the economy? The historical record seems to say so. But this sequence of events is not sufficient evidence for economists, who insist that alternative explanations for the recovery be tested by multiple regression analysis. Unfortunately, the statistical evidence that Netzer would want to see before hopping on the tax cut bandwagon is devilishly difficult to obtain. The outcome of regression studies are split, with some supporting the view that taxes matter, and others finding little evidence.

Netzer is not a complete agnostic on the tax issue, however. Large tax cuts, targeting specific sectors of the economy, can and do make large differences. He cites an analysis of the New York City sales tax through the mid 1960s (when no other government in the metropolitan area had such a tax), showing that the city lost substantial amounts of sales and retail employment because of it. Another quantum change in the tax environment occurred in California after passage of Proposition 13, when counties saw their property tax rates plummet virtually overnight. A careful study of the post-Proposition 13 experience - under conditions almost like those of a laboratory experiment, according to Netzer - revealed significant positive effects for many industries.

Focusing on the dollar costs of tax differentials may miss a larger point, however. Business decisionmakers are swayed as much by the symbolism of tax levels and rates as by their dollar costs. The tax climate, especially the attitude of state officials toward tax cuts, may be the clearest indicator of the overall business climate. Meticulous academic studies in which the tax variable is reduced to dollars and cents, are probably ignoring the variables of greatest concern to businessmen.

8 Interview: Clarence Rappleyea

HL: Let me start by asking you if you see any hope of resolving the state budget questions that we've been dealing with. When you look at the governor's recent statement, you see another $2 billion in taxes, counting, of course, the suspension of the tax cut. You look at the problems we're going to face down the line and you see a $4 billion or $3.5 billion deficit this year, or next year most certainly, and maybe $5 billion the year after that. You start with the assumption that Medicaid spending will continue rising at 17 to 20% per year, and that roughly 40% of your budget is already spent on Medicaid. You don't have to be a mathematical genius to extrapolate that into the future and see Medicaid crowding out other expenses. How can we bring this under control, or can we?

CR: Governor Cuomo talks a great deal about spending caps, but he hasn't demonstrated any real restraint. It's obvious that we don't have a revenue problem here; we have a spending problem. And you've pointed it out yourself-Medicaid and social services are growing at 17% per year. Numbers like this just aren't acceptable. Social services spending now assumes a greater share of the budget than education. As recently as 1983, they were equal. I think that is a terrible thing for this state. As to what's going to happen this time, I don't see any extraordinary chemistry here to change anything. People like the governor have put themselves into a position where they can claim victory if Medicaid growth comes down to somewhere between 12 and 15%. Citizens of this state continue to think that there isn't anything we can do. The fact is, there's a whole lot that can be done by way of restructuring. We should be using more creativity here, not only to curb our spending appetite, but to restructure government, reform service delivery, and explore privatization and other options.

HL: Rapp, where is the consensus to come from on the matter of privatization, or, for that matter, a spending cap or a voucher plan for Medicaid recipients, or any of the reforms that I know you would like to see explored and perhaps embraced. Where is the political consensus to come from?

CR: Unfortunately, the only consensus required to run this state is a consensus of three people: the governor, the majority leader of the Senate, and the speaker of the Assembly. It's rather bizarre to have the whole budget assembled that way. Our budget runs in the neighborhood of between $55 and 60 billion, larger than the national budgets of most countries. I have screamed about the lack of public access to the budget process, and have proposed reforms. Budget-making shouldn't be a back-room deal done by three people. We've got to give people a voice, not only on the budget, but on the total governmental process in New York. That's one of the reasons I'm such a vocal advocate of Initiative and Referendum. It's a tool the people need to fix their government, get into a little "do-it-yourself democracy."

HL: Any chance of getting an issue like referendum? Governor Cuomo continues to talk about it.

CR: Cuomo talks about it in a very limited sense, and I suppose that's the best we're going to get from him. He wants the people to be able to tell the Legislature what to do, but he doesn't want them to have the power to override his vetoes. I would like to see the whole process opened up. The fact that the last two bond propositions were defeated indicates a lot of dissatisfaction with the finances of state government, especially in relation to Cuomo.

ER: You've done a great job on publicizing the things that can be done, including cost-cutting measures that can be introduced, and reforms that you think are necessary. Yet across the state, relatively little is known. We have a job hemorrhage in NYS, where 525,000 jobs have been lost in the last two years. You talk about the indebtedness of this state, which on a per capita basis is the highest in the country. You talk about the combined taxes, the highest in the country, and yet the problems in NY are not as well publicized as the problems in California. When California Governor Pete Wilson called a special emergency meeting of the legislature introducing draconian measures, it got headlines in the *New York Times.* Yet in NY, no one considers the condition of the state's finances to be desperate. So we continue to suffer through this almost incestuous arrangement, where we have a Democratic majority dominating the Assembly, the Republicans controlling the Senate, and a governor who sort of plays both sides like a fine Stradivarius. You have a state in which the media has lost its sense of history. The lack of longevity among most of the press corps means a loss of the capacity to put the state's fiscal condition into historic perspective. As a result, the whole story doesn't get told. Maybe the world we live in doesn't lend itself to deep research, but even things people know about state government don't get reported.

HL: When Hugh Carey was governor, I disagreed with him much of the time. Nonetheless the state was run more efficiently than it's run now, and he was a liberal democrat. Clearly the contrast can be made on non-partisan lines. You compare a liberal democrat of eight years ago and a liberal democrat today, and the philosophy of running this state is different. Carey did *run* this state.

CR: He did. In fact every time I see him I tell him that Mario Cuomo continues to make him look very good. But the fact is, he was a different personality. He might have been labeled a liberal democrat, but he was also a much more practical man, someone who made sure that the balance was better kept. He ran a much tighter ship, largely because, and I think it all boiled down to this, that he empowered his people to act. Mario Cuomo doesn't delegate authority. He does not rely on anyone, nor does he appear to want to rely on anyone. He has a few very close advisors, but beyond that he pretty much calls the shots himself. I think it's methodology more than anything else, that distinguishes Cuomo from Carey.

HL: Carey had one basic philosophical scheme for running this state, very simple and very commonsensical: increases in government expenditure will not exceed the rate of inflation. Cuomo, by contrast, has increased expenditures roughly 13% last year, and in 1994 spending will be up roughly 7%. The smaller increase seems to be a little better than it was in the past, though it's still more than twice the rate of inflation. If you extrapolate out, state government will grow much faster than the private sector, and we're going to simply drive private capital out of NY.

CR: You see it very clearly with the big corporations. In the last 25 years, the number of large corporations headquartered in New York City has declined from 156 to 56. The number of Fortune 500 firms has dropped by one-third in the Cuomo years alone. I'm also concerned about the number of small businesses that we're losing, which no one has on the radar scope at all. We know all about the IBMs, Smith-Coronas, and the Eastman-Kodaks. But it's also the operations with 10 or 20 or 30 or 50 employees that are folding quietly and leaving, or choosing not to start up in NY. It's just too tough an environment. I think that's where we're really taking a hit.

HL: I chatted with Ed Reinfurt who made this same point. Small businesses create most of the new jobs in NY. A small business now has to absorb an additional tax increase, sees the surtax as a permanent part of the economic landscape, and is burdened by more and more state regulation. Businessmen are likely to arrive at the very conclusion that you just mentioned. Why be in NY? What is the incentive to be here? It's just as easy to go across the border into Pennsylvania and New Jersey.

CR: Travelling across the state, it appears that the loss of jobs may be more universal than previously realized. I don't think it's unique to upstate, smaller communities, or to the city. It's generic now. I think that business creation has slowed down visibly-big ones and small ones have gone, are going, or chose not to come.

HL: I give Mario Cuomo his due as a gifted orator and an intelligent guy. Surely he understands the forces driving the other side of the equation of job losses are all those political interests. Surely he knows that trucking firms, for example, are leaving this state at a dramatic rate, and that small businesses are hurting. I'm sure that there are people in the business council who bring this to his attention all the time. Where is the initiative to change things? Is Mario Cuomo simply engaged in the usual circumlocution: Well, I haven't really increased taxes. (You know that's a lie.) Well, I've placed caps on various categories of spending in the state. (That too isn't really true.) How does he explain the problems that we face, the increase in taxation and even his own admission that NY is not doing as well as the rest of the country?

CR: Cuomo insists that we're not the highest taxed state, and he engages in all sorts of *legerdemain* to make that point. He just refuses to acknowledge the obvious, and I find that very troubling because I don't know what force is driving him now. He's certainly been, at best, a caretaker and not a very good one. The *New York Times* recently had an article showing the ten-year record of the Cuomo years. It appears that the thing he is remembered most for, is the number of jail cells he put in place. He says that himself. I find it strange that he is not using this time to really do some dramatic things. Certainly he is an intelligent man, he's got the rhetoric, and very often he talks like a conservative, but he rarely acts like one.

HL: I was on the Alan Chartock program, debating economic reform with the governor, and at the end of the program the governor said: I'm forced to agree with this man, Herb London. I think he's got the right idea. And I was startled because we couldn't possibly be more at odds over the future of this state and what has to be done, and yet at the end of the program he said I agree with the positions that have been espoused by Herb.

CR: Well, he may not only be good with the rhetoric and the intellect, he's good at changing colors. I've seen this over the years, especially when he discusses the budget. And he did it again this year. He said you know Rapp, there are things here that you're probably going to like. Cuomo would have done very well on those wild west medicine wagons, selling potions. He either believes it himself very strongly, or he's deluding himself. I don't know what the answer is, nor do I understand why he would do it that way. As you said, it seems obvious that we are not headed in the right direction.

ER: Perhaps Cuomo thinks the Clinton administration will help the state in a significant way with money? Maybe he's just biding his time until he gets what he thinks he can get from Washington.

CR: That's a possibility, I suppose, but I don't see how that can happen quickly enough. I suppose if the president got the 20 billion job package he's looking for he could infuse some money into the state.

But in the context of a $6 trillion economy, I don't see how that can change the economic outlook in a place as regionalized as New York. And the Clinton administration already seems to be bound up with things that are going to derail their focus on the economy.

ER: Cuomo still blames a lot of the state's problems on so-called withdrawal of federal aid in the last decade, but the numbers don't support that.

CR: All the Reagan-Bush bashing Cuomo's done is belied by the fact that federal aid to New York has been a growing share of New York's budget. When Cuomo became governor, federal aid was one-quarter of our budget. Now it's one-third. So when he blames Washington, he's engaging in the same fallacious reasoning as when he says we are not the heaviest state in taxes. It's syllogism of the worst order that he employs to get to these conclusions.

ER: You mentioned that the problem is spending, not revenues, and I thought you had a letter in the *N.Y. Times* where you gave a concrete example of how the state doesn't even spend the money it has on hand. In other words, how can you possibly blame it on a shortfall of revenues when here we are sitting on piles of money unspent?

CR: Governor Cuomo continues to use borrowing and bonding for all the wrong purposes. I've used the analogy, you've probably seen it, that his debt policy is like taking out a larger mortgage on a house in order to paint it. Cuomo has done this through a lot of one-shots. He has put one-shots in the permanent spending base. We are one of the few states that doesn't put highway user fees and gas tax money into a dedicated fund for infrastructure repair. Cuomo took a lot of things that should have been cut out of the budget entirely and financed them with borrowing, which is wrong. It's no surprise that the last bond issue was shot down by the voters. He employed the one-shot technique when he first got elected and got support then because he convinced everyone that he had inherited a huge debt from the Rockefeller-Wilson era. At that time, he said that after he got this infusion of money by the transportation bond, he would cut out the practice. But the infrastructure constantly kept eroding, and we're now at a point where it's very difficult to catch up. But, again, it's the same as the lottery.

The public was sold on the notion that the lottery was going to be used to supplement education. In fact, it only displaced some of the annual budget funds for education. It became a shell game, with Cuomo's hands moving faster than the taxpayers' eyes.

Commentary: HL

There is bipartisan accord on the need to mobilize political support for reform in New York State. One of the Republican point men in this effort is "Rapp" Rappleyea, the minority leader in the Assembly and among the most consistent reform-minded leaders on the Republican side of the aisle. It was Rapp who noted that as late as 1991, the percentage of social services and Medicaid in the budget was the equivalent of educational expenditures. By 1993, however, the former expenses were 41 percent of the budget, while education remained static at 28 percent. Recognizing this disparity as corrosive, Rapp called for "restructuring" and the privatization of many state services.

Yet calls for restructuring, even during the dark days of budget reconciliation, are like whistles during a storm at sea. Someone is calling for help; it just can't be heard amid the din. The secrecy surrounding budget construction and the inattentiveness to privatization proposals (such as the Lauder commission) militate against any significant state reforms. By all accounts, Cuomo's fiscal methodology is insulated from legislative review. Perhaps that explains the rancor surrounding the budget process.

Most significantly, as Assemblyman Rappleyea and others interviewed for this book have indicated, the environment for business activity has turned rancid. It isn't only the well-publicized departure of companies like I.B.M. and Key Bank, it's the departure of Mom and Pop operations that never make the local newspapers. Burdened by high corporate taxes, "temporary" surtaxes that are never lifted, and rigid regulations that escalate the price of doing business, small firms are told directly and indirectly that they aren't welcome in New York State. An assessment of corporate net income tax burden as a percentage of the national average places New York State in first place, 98 percent above the national average. And interestingly, on the matter of state and local spending per capita, New York is in second place - surpassed only by Alaska - and is 52 percent above the national average. Clearly, the Cuomo legacy is not the attraction of private capital.

Despite all of the governor's rhetorical flourishes, his charge that the budgetary problems of New York State lie at the doorstep of Presidents Reagan and Bush won't stand up to careful scrutiny. Since 1983 - Cuomo's first year as governor - federal revenue sharing has increased from $6 billion to $18 billion, a three hundred percent increase in eleven years. Any way you slice it, that's "real" money. Obviously it isn't enough to meet the states' insatiable appetite for spending, but my guess is that if the federal government allocated more money, New York State would spend more money.

Rather than deal directly with trying to curb spending in New York, Cuomo has decided to find loopholes in the State Constitution which arguably permit "one shots" and back-door borrowing. These practices are tantamount to changing the ownership of your car to your spouses's name and then contending that you have $20,000 of disposable income. Surely the practice of taking state assets and selling them to state agencies where they are converted into bonds is questionable, at the very least. Moreover, a dedicated fund, such as the dedicated highway fund, is an oxymoron. All funds in the state are used to balance the budget.

Can these questionable practices continue? Unfortunately the magnitude of the state debt isn't well understood, nor do most New Yorkers realize that a significant portion of their tax dollars go to pay the interest on that debt. Since New York has the lowest bond rating of any state in the nation, interest rates must be high to attract bond buyers; taxpayers are left holding the bag. Yet with the exception of a few journalists who have emphasized this point, the story remains largely untold.

Perhaps the next gubernatorial campaign will allow for a careful examination state finances, but I am not sanguine that will be the case. When so many New Yorkers have a stake in present practices, there is a greater likelihood that the reality will be denied than that the reality will be exposed. But the financial signs are apparent to many New Yorkers: People are leaving the state at a record pace, businesses cannot be attracted nor can they be encouraged to remain, signs of tax-base erosion are evident, and basic services are languishing.

Yet the story hasn't been told effectively enough to influence the man-on-the-street. That is the task that lies ahead.

9 Interview: Edward Regan

(Interview conducted in February 1993. At the time Ned Regan was the Comptroller of New York State.)

NR: You know all the problems. The legislature offers no real resistance to the Governor's spending proposal. Their budget plans are as bad as the Governor's, full of one-shots and other gimmicks. And incumbency is a problem: the voters are upset because so many senators and the assemblymen were reelected, despite widespread unhappiness with the tax and spend policies they've enacted. They just routinely seem to be returned to office. The Governor is routinely returned office too. The 1990 election was a fluke, though you know much much more about it than I. In my opinion, you, Herb, would be governor if half of the Republicans had given you an endorsement. Ironically, the guy who prevented that, Pat Barrett, had he run himself as he said he would, would be governor today. Pat's disappearance in the key months of January, February, March, April & May, left Roy Goodman and Larry Leeds to make the decision out of their Rolodex file.

HL: While it may be impossible to discuss monumental change, let's just say at the margin, we can talk about some modest improvements in the State of New York.

NR: Let me tell you what I think may be the core reason that militates against change; it's an accident, it wasn't designed, it wasn't created and it can't be undone. The elements of it are this: the New York City newspapers, and electronic media, with only rare exceptions, never mention the names of the New York State senators and assemblymen. There are over a hundred legislators, but we don't know what they're doing. Anyone can pick up a newspaper and find out what New York City's mayor stands for. In Albany, the important issues are hammered out in the back-room, with only the Governor and legislative leaders in attendance.

If you want to turn things around, and this is not in the interest of the legislative leaders, you have to find out what your own legislator stands for. The fact is that few newspapers in the state (except the *Syracuse Post Standard* and *The Albany Times Union*) cover state affairs thoroughly. City Hall is put under a microscope. Albany might as well be out in Idaho. A recent poll shows that the readers are hungry for details about the shenanigans in Albany. They suspect it's bad, but they don't know how bad because they are not told.

ER: Well, Mario Cuomo is certainly a darling of the media.

NR: I'm not sure about that. Somewhere along the line Cuomo became an unpopular guy. Again, he could have easily lost for governor, easily lost if you were the Republican nominee, instead of Pierre Rinfret. The Republican leadership dropped the ball on that one.

ER: The point is that anyone that cared to investigate his history could have uncovered Rinfret's deficiencies.

NR: I knew about him. We had spoken on a program together. But who took the time to investigate? You were down to three days before the Republican convention in Rye Town Hilton, and the rest is history. But Cuomo was enormously unpopular then and he is today. The media favor him more than they should but I personally don't think he's their darling. There are a lot of negative articles. The *New York Times* writes negative stories about the Governor and the editorials are negative too, if you look back at them. But the *New York Times* has never printed that the credit rating in New York State is number fifty out of fifty states. It is the worst state in the country. Our budget went up far more, adjusting for inflation, than did the City of New York. Albany disguised it somewhat by shuffling the current operating budget into the capital budget. UDC, the Urban Development Center, for example, is a sloppy borrower. It has no discipline in what it does. A few years ago New York State "sold" Attica prison to UDC for $200 million. UDC sold 30-year bonds to pay for the prison. Albany called it "revenues", but no one seemed to care. It goes on and on. The problem is that journalists don't like math. I think the papers in this town, in this state, while they give superb coverage to City Hall and Washington, simply have decided you're never going to hear much about Albany.

ER: I think part of the problem is that the state budget is so complex.

HL: The off-budget expenditures and the increase in off-budget expenditures are clear indications of its complexity and it's simply hard to get control over what's going on.

NR: Newspaper editors don't want you to know. The budget is complex on purpose. When I tell the editors that I will name names, about who is manipulating the budget, the newspaper editors yawn. That's just the simple fact. So as I've suggested, in this state there's a real difficulty. Having said this, I believe there can be a credible campaign for governor. You can certainly bring home the message that Cuomo's message is misguided. I don't see how professional journalists can ignore a strong candidate. A very strong campaign for governor can get issues discussed. Unfortunately, state finances are a yawn for most newspapers.

ER: Are these things unique to New York? The lack of media coverage?

NR: Sure, it's unique to a large major urban area that has the U.N. At any one time there are five U.S. Senators and three Governors in this city and there are several presidents of countries. There's no way the press can cover this city; there's no way the press will put the state ahead of all other concerns. There's no way they can print every assemblyperson's name. There's just too much going on. If it were Chicago, of course, an assemblyman would get his name in now and then, and a comptroller most definitely. The media is a terror there. You have to keep in mind, that with the exception of Channel 12 on Long Island, few people in this state know about their assemblymen from television. In New York there's no way they can know. It's not anybody's fault, much as I think the press ought to focus more on Albany's finances than it does.

HL: I think you've raised some interesting points, and the gubernatorial campaign, at least from the experience I've had, transcends what happens in the media. That is, by virtue of your participation in a campaign, the dynamics are changed. Suppose you leave personalities out of it and some fellow or woman runs for governor of New York who is capable of articulating the issues. Assume this person runs with a mandate for economic reform in New York and gets elected. What are the prospects for change when someone comes to Albany with a reform agenda on the table? Will he still face the resistance that you referred to in the Assembly and the Senate? Will this person be ignored by the *New York Times* and the other media outlets in New York state?

NR: No. There might not be resistance. I said the normal way to get your program through is to get a senator or assemblyman to go along with it. That will be covered in Syracuse, and maybe by a few of the local newspapers in other cities. But in New York City? Forget it. Major elected officials (with the exception of the Mayor and Governor) are never on the radio, never on t.v. and never in the newspapers.

HL: Let me raise a rather ticklish subject: we who have been associated with Change-New York have been excoriated because we reveal the voting record of people in the Assembly and the Senate. If you look at the documents we have produced, I'd say well over 90% are nothing more than a statement of voting records, and an attempt to compare the oratory of people running for office with their voting record in the Senate and Assembly.

NR: See, I can't even get that from the press corps, with the exception of Syracuse. Not once did they think it was of any interest to their readers to find out how their senators or assemblymen vote, or they don't want to embarrass the incumbent. They don't think it sells newspapers.

HL: Let's say you are facing the prospect of a genuine emergency, and people will recognize a financial emergency, when you are four billion dollars in the hole. Let's say there are very few resources left in the state to sell; I mean how many prisons remain? What else are you going to do with your canal system? How do you resolve this crisis?

NR: Oh, the imagination of these people in Albany! Don't worry about it.

HL: OK, let's say I'm underestimating their imagination and their other schemes. Nonetheless, you've got, according to Standard & Poor's the lowest bond rating, and according to Moody's, the second lowest bond rating in the United States. That's a big cost to the taxpayers.

NR: I've not gotten one newspaper to print your simple statement. Now there might be an exception here or there. But when the bond downgrading happened it wasn't news. I never got any coverage at all, even in the *New York Times*. There was one story and that was buried.

ER: But the *Times* was against the "jobs" bond issue.

NR: Yes, but for other reasons. I wanted to use the bond issue as a vehicle to attack state finances. My point is this, that I wanted to use the bond issue as an expression against fiscal malpractice. I did get a column in the *Daily News* about this matter only after I crashed a press conference (held on Long Island) held by Richard Kessel. I walked in and said I'm not going to let you stonewall me on this issue. I got good coverage. I drove home the point and I helped sink a bond issue that was probably going to pass. It was a huge defeat for Cuomo. I didn't care about the bond, heck we probably needed the jobs. Nobody disagrees to a little stimulant at the right moment. The right stimulant at the right moment in the economy is good. Sometimes you need a hot poker to get the thing going at the right place and the right time. But I used the bond issue as a vehicle to criticize the state's policy of using debt to pay for current spending. It never really got any kind of coverage here in the city. In fact, the areas where the bond issue lost were in the areas my position got good coverage.

HL: How do you see the budget unfolding this year then? Do you think it's going to be Mario pulling a rabbit out of a hat?

NR: Well I don't know, the governor has come out very strongly in favor of the program to eliminate the state's practice of back-door borrowing. Again, zero coverage here in this city and even in *Newsday*. I spent an hour with a reporter Tuesday and the story has yet to appear.

Cuomo came out very strongly for reform in the way the state borrows money. He made it the centerpiece of the State of the State address. He and I then went before the annual meeting of the New York State Bankers' Association and laid out the Constitutional Amendments that we're going to introduce. They'll all be introduced on Tuesday. This represents a total change in the way we borrow. So at this point I don't see how he could support more backdoor borrowing.

ER: What are the Constitutional changes?

NR: Well, the changes are to close the backdoor, no more borrowing by remote authorities, no more middle of the night deals, no more lease purchase debt, no more moral obligation debt. Borrowing for bricks and mortar projects only. Our debt should consist either of self-liquidating revenue bonds, or General Obligation (G.O.) tax-supported bonds that have been put on the ballot and approved by the voters. The fact that you have to ask about this reform is just amazing. Here we are fifty out of fifty, or forty-nine out of fifty, in the bond ratings, because we borrow in obscure ways and no one knows about it. The governor opened up his State of the State address with this issue and still there hasn't been a major story on it.

ER: This is bad stuff. There are many wealthy people in New York State who benefit from tax exempt state paper. That's why Albany can sell these bonds at competitive rates. I think they're insulated from this fiscal madness.

NR: Yes, all they care about is the interest rate. Well at any rate, the tide has turned. We can't rely on gimmicks any longer.

HL: That was the implication of my remark when I asked how the budget was going to unfold. I'm aware of what was said in the State of the State.

NR: I have no idea how the budget will unfold. It's probably a two billion dollar problem. Cuomo is cutting everybody across the board ten percent and there will be a lot of deferrals and that sort of stuff. I don't know what the answer is, I have to wait and see. I don't do any real budget analysis. When we write about the budget we disaggregate all the phony stuff in it, and in two pages tell you what's really going on. Cuomo won't do that. For real trends you have to aggregate all the major revenues and spending categories, and compare them to the preceding years.

HL: When does your statement come out?

NR: We don't do that until well into the budget year. But the press could care less. The fact is that the only time the press uses this is to chase Cuomo around and needle him in a press conference. But they won't write about it. I don't care if they go after Cuomo as long as they print something but they won't.

ER: When the state has cut budgets its usually been on the backs of school districts and local governments. State taxes aren't that high in New York, but the state has shifted the burden to local governments. I'm talking about mandates such as Medicaid, special education, courts, and many others.

NR: This government has mistreated localities as you well know Ed, more than any other state. The way Albany works is very clear: it's gain here, pain there. It's gain in Albany and pain in Yonkers or New York City and the Medicaid bill obviously being the most, but not the only, egregious example. Its gain here and the pain is fifteen years later when you're paying the debt service for all these borrowings made to balance the budget. It's always the same pattern, shift responsibility to another government, shift from the operating budgets to the capital budget. You shift the gain this year for the ribbon cutting ceremonies and the rebuilding effort and spread the pain out over time.

ER: I'm doing a piece on the city's budget for the *City Journal*. As you know, the city claims that it doesn't get its share of state education aid. It gets all the mandates for children with disabilities, special ed, the hard to educate, but not enough funding.

NR: I don't get in to that in much detail. It could very well be. The pattern in Albany was hardly invented by Mario Cuomo. It's been the pattern there for ages. It's always to blur accountability. They point to somebody else and the legislators pretend to squawk about the leadership and the way the system works.

ER: I think the leadership thing is the media thing; only a few people in state government call the shots. They are the ones who get their names in the paper. The rest of the crew has no choice but to go along.

NR: That goes with the territory. For instance, in the few stories that have been written about budget reform, Cuomo being lavishly generous in giving me credit for the whole thing, my role was virtually ignored.

HL: That's the way the press interprets accountability.

NR: Presumably all the reporters thought that they had covered me enough in the bond campaign. They wrote that I had attacked the bond issue and handed Cuomo a defeat. They're not going to bother printing another story. Did you know that New York City had a surplus this year? Because of my idea. The bill I helped pass to end spring borrowing took ten years to enact. New York City finally got paid by the state on time. Of course the story didn't appear anywhere. Dinkins is publicly giving me credit, Cuomo is publicly giving me credit, the financial control board is publicly giving me credit, but not one line has ever appeared anywhere. I know it goes with the territory, but it's frustrating for me and my staff.

ER: Would the new method of finance--ending the spring borrowing--reduce the structural deficit of New York City, or is that simply a one-time timing change?

NR: Well, it's a huge timing change. New York City will get $800 million when it needs it, not six months later as is the case now. Probably its budget impact is one-time only.

ER: I haven't seen that in the newspapers.

NR: Never. What they do say is that the stock market, that Wall Street has responded favorably to the state payment schedule.

ER: Wall street is bringing in a lot more revenue. Perhaps that's why you have a surplus in New York City.

NR: What you have to think about is how come Perot got whatever vote he got in this state? We defeated the bond act, but every-body--the good guys and the bad guys--are routinely returned to office. How come you see polls that show great voter unhappiness with state government, that there's a "revolt" and yet they didn't get us.

HL: Well I think Cuomo should be commended for the constitutional reform, for accepting the proposal. The question that immediately comes to mind is here's a man who has been governor for eleven years, yet we have a constitutional reform occurring now. Why not six years ago, seven years ago?

NR: I don't think you're going to get a chance to debate Cuomo. My instincts tell me, he will not run for another term. If it's a candidate out of the Senate or Assembly, that's another matter. I know that there are a lot more candidates for governor on the Republican side than there are on the Democratic side. It's a very interesting switch.

Commentary: HL

As I turn the pages of the major New York City and statewide newspapers, I'm struck by the lack of news emanating from Albany. There is the usual political gossip. But rarely does a story appear that deals with a hardhitting analysis of state finances. In fact, the most extensive state story to appear in the *New York Times* in the last year dealt with Mario Cuomo's penchant for basketball playing.

It was therefore not particularly surprising to hear Ned Regan say that the press corps routinely ignores state matters. Albany may not be Idaho--to use Mr. Regan's turn of phrase--but it is in the nether reaches of the state beyond the ken of the typical reporter whose eyes are fixed on New York City or Washington, D.C.

It is certainly instructive that it is rarely reported that New York State has the lowest bond rating of the fifty states. Perhaps even more instructive is that I haven't read one newspaper account which spells out the meaning of a low bond rating for taxpayers. Nor is the budgetary trick of collapsing a portion of the current operating budget into the capital budget an issue which the press explicates.

While Mr. Regan is certainly right in arguing that New York is a mecca for international and national events and personalities which often crowd out state issues, I'm convinced he is wrong in his general analysis of the state press corps. Mario Cuomo didn't invent an uninterested state press team. It has always been hard to tell the New York State story. Many factors contribute to this condition, including the intentional anonymity of state senators and assemblymen who, with rare exceptions, do the bidding of their leaders, the majority leader and the speaker.

Yet if an article can be written about Cuomo's basketball playing, surely an article can be written about Cuomo's management of the state. The problem is that the opposition party doesn't fully realize that press reports are predigested tales, stories written for reporters with the eyecatching headline and the opening paragraph. Newspaper accounts aren't generally written, they are reproduced.

Therefore, stories about changes in borrowing procedures are not reported because the press corps regards them as boring. Take the same story and put it in the context of state assets like Attica Prison and the Aqueduct Parking Lot that have been sold to an agency of government, the Urban Development Corporation, in order to meet the mandated state budget and, *voila*, you have a story with sex appeal. Unfortunately, the opposition party doesn't understand this matter as it should and the stories emanating out of Albany have a distinctively gray tone to them.

It should be recalled that the state comptroller has the authority to bring the government to a grinding halt. The governor must seek his approval for the budget. If that budget isn't genuinely balanced, the comptroller can say so. Similarly, he has the authority to blow the whistle on questionable budget practices at the county level and he must attest to the financial integrity of the state pension. Hence the comptroller, notwithstanding Ned Regan's view to the contrary, can make news.

Can you imagine the brouhaha if the comptroller refuses to sign the governor's budget, assuming he considers its numbers a phony expression of fiscal reality? Surely the press corps would notice. The spin on a story where one person has the courage to stand up to the lumbering state bureaucracy has all the elements of a successful Hollywood film. Yet in my memory, no one has sought this role or considered it an appropriate exercise of power.

In the last analysis, the press is as good as the people about whom it reports. Those shying away from stories that may embarrass them are obviously not candidates for profiles. Those issues interred in arcane debate or discussed at 2 a.m. beyond the glare of klieg lights are certainly not going to be front page stories. The news isn't manipulated, but it is suggested. As long as the powers that be don't suggest the stories that may capture the public's imagination, Albany will remain a backwater, eliciting little interest.

10 Interview: Edward Reinfurt

(Interview Conducted in February 1993; budget under discussion is the 1993 budget)

HL: Why don't you start by giving us your assessment of where the state budget stands, where it's likely to go, how things are going to come out, and then, if you could look at this in some sort of larger context, give us your view of the future of New York. Can it be saved? And if so, how?

Ed Reinfurt: New York can only be saved if it has a growing economy. If we do nothing to stimulate the economy, growth of state spending will far exceed our personal income growth for sometime to come. People are reluctantly realizing that tax hikes cannot solve the budget problem. There's this growing perception of 'hold it, we said four years ago that this is a temporary problem, why do we still have problems when each year we're anteing up an additional billion dollars or two, additional taxes and fees?' And quickly you conclude that spending cuts are the only viable alternative. And clearly the Medicaid budget is driving state spending.

On the revenue side, corporate collections are up significantly, but sales and use taxes are totally flat, which means that people are not spending more because they're earning less. The personal income numbers have shown below average growth, but at least it's growth. But it's not the growth we had when our economy was booming in the early 1980s. And what we have to realize is that we have to get our economy going again.

It's frustrating to look at this budget and look at the economic assumptions, which basically say that New York will grow less rapidly than the rest of the country. I don't think we as a state should accept that. To me, that is the number one challenge of this budget, next year's budget, the budget after that. How do we turn this economy around? From a budgeting standpoint, I think no one is faulting the assumption of slow growth. It is conservative, it probably is right, it has been certainly right for the last few years. But what are we doing about that? Are we willing to accept not only slow growth for the next decade, but trailing the rest of the country? To me, and I think to increasing numbers of New Yorkers, the answer is no. That's our challenge.

Ed Rubenstein: I was just going to say, I think, and correct me if I'm wrong, that the fiscal problem has deteriorated to the point where even if the economy does come back a la the 1980's, there will still be problems. You cannot grow your way out of this. We have to, I think, make fundamental cuts in things that up to this point have not been addressed seriously. I would certainly put Medicaid entitlement on the table, not just as state assumption from the local governments, but for a reduction in the scope of this entitlement. I think the economy is important but I don't think it's going to solve the fiscal problem of New York State.

Ed Reinfurt: I agree, and I would like to take a few minutes and talk about Medicaid. There is one thing I want to stress--that the debate on Medicaid tends to get bogged down on whether someone should have x-type of care, or the number of hours of home care, or dental, or whatever. We tend to get into these comparisons between what we spend in New York versus California versus other states. What policy makers should be looking at, however, is the tremendous disparity in what we spend within New York State, county versus county. We have per capita expenditures that differ by 6 to 1, from one county to another. And we're not talking about people being sicker in one county than another; we're looking at a system where hospital care is more expensive in one county than another. If someone would focus on why there are these tremendous disparities, you could begin to learn a lot about cost control.

I wish more people would spend time looking at why is it that in Monroe County, Medicaid expenditures are basically 60% of the state average, but when you go to Erie County, directly to the west, the number shoots up, and when you go east to Onondaga County, the number also shoots up. You can do that all over the state. What we're not asking is "why?"

It is more than simply an issue of cost. There are certain admission patterns, diagnostic patterns, and other aspects of Medicaid that differ greatly county by county. It may be that this pattern reflects serious public health problems in some areas. If so, we should know that, and address that. From a public policy standpoint, it's something to look at.

HL: Is that really the case? My suspicion, Ed, is that what you see may reflect the extent to which the municipal unions have affected employment patterns in hospitals and nursing homes in the various counties. If you were to look at this county by county, you would find a political dimension to these decisions, and that in fact costs can be controlled. I mean, I think your analysis is correct and that it's a good idea to look at this county by county, and to look at the disparities and to ask why the differences exist. But I suspect that rather than a health crisis, you would find the answers more readily if you were to look at the political dimensions of this question.

Ed Reinfurt: I think you're right. You can look particularly at the personal care expenditures and make that case. Because what you find is a tremendous growth in home health care, and the assumption is that we're taking care of people who would have otherwise been in a hospital or a skilled nursing home. If true, this would be an efficient use of Medicaid funds. But the numbers don't show that. It shows that we're treating the same number of individuals in hospitals and nursing homes, and our costs are going up at a tremendous rate.

I have some comparisons of ten year growth in Medicaid expenditures by the type of care: total medical expenditures went up 213 percent. That's alarming, but when you get into the components, you'll see home health care in that period has gone up 866 percent. And if you do three-year comparisons, because there wasn't a lot of home health care ten years ago, you've got home care up by 149%. And where you really want to see growth--in people seeing physicians--is the smallest growing part of Medicaid. So we're not inducing people to seeing doctors as we should. We spend appallingly little on physicians compared to the rest of the country, because we have this low reimbursement rate for physicians services.

On the other hand, there are some success stories: we had runaway laboratory and x-ray cost five years ago, they've gone down 52% in the last five years. That's positive. But we're not putting the same attention in other areas.

Ed Rubenstein: Couldn't the county to county variation be a function of the location of nursing homes, because that's really the biggest expense.

Ed Reinfurt: It could be. But just look at the hospital variations. We haven't added a lot of nursing homes in this state in the last five or ten years. So the growth in skilled nursing compared to the other Medicaid costs is relatively modest.

The costs of skilled nursing home care have grown 53% in the last three years, which is modest compared to others components of Medicaid.

HL: Let me come back to the question that you raised just a moment ago on x-rays and laboratory costs going down. What precisely accounted for this decrease?

Ed Reinfurt: Efforts were made to control utilization, such as requiring prior approval--prior approval if, I believe, you went beyond a single x-ray. Once the system was set up to look at what is appropriate, then things began to change. X-rays and lab costs in 1988 were $208 million; in 1991, the last available year for comparisons, it fell to $65 million.

You can't blame the explosion in Medicaid spending on the medical inflation rate. For example, the cost of transporting Medicaid patients to hospitals and doctors has gone up 52% in the last three years. What's the transportation inflation rate? Is there something unique? So, you see you can't just blame it on medical costs generally.

Ed Rubenstein: The ambulance corp is a very powerful lobbyist in New York City. They are on the Medicaid take.

HL: So you would think it would have gone up at a rate even higher than Medicaid?

Ed Rubenstein: Perhaps.

HL: Your main point is that if a careful microanalysis were done of medical costs county by county, there would be a lot of intriguing things to look at, and a lot of cost containment measures that could be introduced. So presumably the goal is to start looking at what we're doing county by county so that we can implement state-wide cost containment measures.

Ed Reinfurt: That's right.   If you look at county figures on managed care, you'll get some very encouraging results in terms of quality and cost. The latest numbers for enrollment show that we only have 7.5% of those who are eligible in a managed care setting, although, some counties are doing very well. The county of Chemung, for example has 48% of its eligible population in a managed care facility--2100 people out of 4500. That's impressive, especially if you look at the dollar savings that are beginning to show up between managed care program enrolees and their control group, a group similarly situated with regard to age and health condition. I would say managed care is between 15 and 20 percent cheaper.

But the important thing is for everyone to know what this means. Many counties have doctors participating in managed care. Rensselaer county was successful in recruiting dozens of new physicians into a managed care program. And so you have a positive thing taking place where people are seeing doctors. In Buffalo, where the pilot program was in place, it was not only cost-effective but more importantly, it was providing a much higher quality of care.

Ed Rubenstein: Are private sector HMOs provided for in these county plans?

Ed Reinfurt: Almost always.

Ed Rubenstein: So basically, counties now contract-out Medicaid directly to the private sector.

Ed Reinfurt: Yes, in the case of Rensselaer county, I think they went with Wellcare. But I'm looking at a whole list of providers. You have Metropolitan in one, Elder Plan in another, US Healthcare, etc.... So it's either a private plan, or an HMO, or a doctor consortium.

Ed Rubenstein: And are the benefits available to people in these HMO's the same in all parts of the state?

Ed Reinfurt: Identical. In order to be qualified as a Medicaid provider you have to offer all the services that a Medicaid recipient is entitled to.

The difference from traditional Medicaid is the limits put on access by the HMO. Someone in the HMO looks at the appropriateness of service.

Ed Rubenstein: I know that the state had pilot projects years ago, in the early or mid-1980s, that never worked out. For some reason the private HMOs never were happy with state reimbursement rates.

HL: And yet the results here are clearly suggestive of a significant quantitative change, and you're suggesting even a qualitative change.
Ed Reinfurt: What we're talking about are some early successes with managed care. It is a significant change.

Ed Rubenstein: I'd like to see those numbers, because I haven't seen the actual HMO results. This is something that has happened in the last year or so. It's heartening.

HL: Come back to the growth side of the equation for a minute. What would you do to get more growth in New York? Is it the elimination of the mandates, is it the elimination of taxes, corporate taxes?

Ed Reinfurt: First, I think you have to understand where your growth is going to come from. The headlines only tell you the story of the big guys downsizing, and that's going to occur in this state and in this nation. If you ask most people, what is the role of small business today, there's this misconception of how many jobs they provide. They are by far the largest provider of jobs. Still, many are dependent on their contracts with larger businesses or with the employees of larger businesses. Firms with fewer than 50 employees account for 41% of the workforce; those with over 1000, the big guys, only account for 17%. And this is where the perception is so important. Because when that small employer is struggling to make a payroll, or to pay health insurance, and he is hit with another fee or another tax, he doesn't have the public forum to say 'state government, help me.' Nor does he expect it. He's going to go where he is wanted, or where he thinks he can have a better chance to succeed, and that's what we've got to be nervous about, and thinking of. What does this do for the small employer? The test of any budget question is, 'is it good for the economy or isn't it?' And if you can't say 'it is' you can't afford to take that step.

HL: And yet the steps have been taken routinely. An industry that I know quite a bit about, the trucking industry, having a very significant and prominent role in the western part of the state, particularly in Erie county, has been leaving for Pennsylvania in droves, roughly a 100 firms leaving a year.

Ed Reinfurt: A lot of it is the cost of diesel fuel.

HL: Diesel fuel is part of it. You take one of these big trucks and put it on the New York State Thruway, it's 22 cents a mile to run the truck, on the Pennsylvania Turnpike, it's 5 cents.

Ed Reinfurt: It's a dramatic difference. You don't have to think too hard about that.

HL: You want to circumvent New York, it's very easy, just go right around the southern tier, come right up to New York City. You don't have to be in New York State.

Ed Reinfurt: People say 'ah, that's not true. Truckers have to come through New York.'
     If you want to look at a classic impact of New York's regulatory structure and what it does, look at Lifecare communities for seniors. Four years ago, with great fanfare, we announced that New York is going to have a program, a structure, a statute to deal with Lifecare communities. We've got a lot of wealthy seniors, moderately well-off, who want to downsize their house, live in a different type of environment. This is not funded by Medicaid or any of those programs. This is totally private. What we did in New York was to put in place the most stringent regulations as to reserve requirements for anyone building this development. As a result, we have still not built a single Lifecare facility in New York State. And these things are going on all around the country. Seniors in other states have the opportunity to buy housing. Look at what it means in terms of construction jobs, in terms of keeping New Yorkers here. And that's not theory, that's a real factor in the economy.

Ed Rubenstein: That's understood by a large portion of the population out there. It tweaks the demographic movement.

HL: Have you written about that? The Lifecare issue is a great story. That's a wonderful metaphor for the entire state.

Ed Reinfurt: We have to protect our citizens; instead, what the state managed to do is protect them from having a home. Maybe this year we'll look at privatizing the state insurance fund.

Ed Rubenstein: But the money that you get from privatizing will be blown on more state spending. We're all fearful of what the state is going to do with the money. What about the recent budget? It got pretty high marks in the press I think, relative to the other budgets that we've seen. What is your read on that?

Ed Reinfurt: If you look at the 1993 budget and ask what is in there that is good for the economy and that will stimulate it, you don't find much. People who have been getting hit over the head for the last four years will say 'the pounding isn't any worse, the fifth round is the same as the first, and I'm not getting beat any worse,' That's in part why I think you don't see more of a backlash. Because there really weren't a lot of new things, and that's good because we don't need another new tax.

But we don't also need to permanently retain some of the surcharges that were put place in the past to deal with a temporary fiscal problem. If we say we need to make them permanent, then we're saying we have a permanent fiscal problem. We think that's the wrong message to send to small businesses. Part of the recovery process is that you have hope that things are going to get better, the confidence factor. It doesn't give business people any confidence if you tell them we're going to give you a permanent surcharge.

HL: Especially when you consider the way in which the surcharge was introduced. Was it 15% the first year, 15% the second, then zero?

Ed Reinfurt: Ten percent the second year.

HL: What you are saying, and you're delivering a very profound message to businesses across the state, is if there's a surcharge and it's called temporary, it's a lie. That's an oxymoron, there's no such thing as a temporary surcharge. It can be very discerning.

Ed Reinfurt: It's like a temporary increase in the income tax.

HL: I remember the promises, I remember the governor saying ' I assure you this is temporary, this is really temporary.'

Ed Rubenstein: What about the cost of Workers' Compensation and the numbers that you came up with?

Ed Reinfurt: Oh yes, that is an issue that we've got to get serious about. The increases in Workers' Compensation, a mandated program in this state and every state, is totally paid for by employers. The cost of that is currently $5 billion, the same as we're paying in total business taxes. This is a major cost of doing business in New York State.

HL: Five billion dollars? I thought it was $3 billion.

Ed Reinfurt: Five billion dollars. It's a mandate totally paid by business. What we're trying to propose this year is to allow for managed care in the Workers' Compensation, same thing we're talking about Medicaid. We have to do it in fairness to employers as well as employees. The medical cost of Workers' Compensation, when you're injured on the job your Blue Cross does not pay for it, it's your Workers' Compensation dollar that pays for your rehabilitation. Thirty-eight cents out of every Workers' Compensation dollar is the medical component. It is the fastest growing component. It's in addition to the indemnity benefit we give to the worker for being out of work. The medical side is growing at 17% a year. And as with Medicaid, we have all these variations in Workers' Compensation.

A number of people down in Albany think that health care reform is about getting more money to the hospitals. They're missing the point. We've got to understand what's going on in our health care system, whether it's in the Medicaid component or the non-Medicaid. We've got to have it make sense. We currently have what we like to call a health care field of dreams, where the belief is that if you provide a service, someone will pay for it. And the fact is that the people who have been paying, the businesses and the governments, are saying 'NO!'

That field of dreams is over. Just because you have a shingle doesn't mean you have free access to my insurance money. And that is what the debate over health care has to be about. And from a public policy standpoint, you have all these arguments over universal care, we've been saying 'look, we're 90% of the way there in terms of medical care. Between what the private sector provides its employees and what the public provides for the neediest, nine out of 10 New Yorkers are covered. We need to address the other ten percent, but we're never going to be able to afford the other ten unless we get the 90 percent under control.' And that's the real challenge. Speaking today, just to wrap this up, we're saying 'yes, you need to look at fiscal policies and make the right decisions. You need to look at your taxes, health care, and Workers' Compensation. Those three are the three biggest areas. And in there, there should be a partnership, because what's driving the tax decisions are the health decisions and the Medicaid. So you can't ignore the big picture, you can't tinker around the edges any longer. Those days are over.

Commentary: ER

In February 1993 New York state quietly passed an important economic milestone. The number of manufacturing jobs in the state dropped below 1 million for the first time since about 1906. The bad news followed nearly three decades of decline, during which the number of industrial jobs fell by more than half.

As Vice President of the Business Council, the state's largest business association, Ed Reinfurt has studied this problem in depth. Some of the job loss, he believes, reflects an industrial base that has become more productive--producing more goods with fewer workers. But this cannot explain why New York has done so much worse than the rest of the country:

New York's Never Ending Recession

	NYS	Rest of Nation
---- Total Payroll Jobs ---- (in Millions)		
May 1990	8.264	101.519
July 1990	8.225	101.476
March 1991	7.953	100.411
February 1994	7.766	103.366
---- Percent Change ----		
May 1990 to March 1991:	-3.8%	-1.1%
March 1991 to Feb. 1994:	-2.4	2.6

Source: NYS Department of Labor.

From the peak of the 1980s boom (May 1990) to the trough of the 1991 recession, employment declined 3.8% in New York State, and 1.1% in the rest of the nation. Since March 1991, however, employment has risen by 2.1% in the rest of the nation, but has declined by 3.2% in New York.

Something clearly is rotten in the State of New York.

Every time the Business Council has surveyed its membership, the higher cost of doing business here is the major factor cited for the statewide job losses.

The tax problem has been well documented. New York State and its local governments collected an average $3,337 in taxes from every resident in 1991--$1,200 more than the national average and $500 more per capita than the next ranking states, Hawaii, New Jersey, and Connecticut. More importantly, Albany derives a disproportionate share of its total tax take from personal income taxes. A higher PIT means that wages must also be higher in New York, which automatically boosts production costs.

High taxes, however, do not necessarily drive business away. Minnesota, a relatively high tax state, has been successful in attracting firms, while low-cost Mississippi has not. The disincentives of high taxes can be offset by efficient public services, or by reducing government regulations and business mandates.

Unfortunately, these mitigating factors are absent here.

Data collected by the U.S. Census Bureau show that New York's state and local governments spent an average of $5,963 per capita in 1991. This was second (to Alaska), and 52% above the national average. Even when measured against New York's above average income, our government spends more than all but three other states.

Government payrolls remain bloated, with 622 state and local government employees per 10,000 population in New York State, versus 523 in the nation as a whole. Government employees have, in effect, crowded out private sector workers. In 1990, for example, there were 30% more government jobs than manufacturing jobs in New York State, compared to a national disparity between these groups of only 6.2%.

Education and social services account for nearly 60% of the budget. The fastest growing state budget item--and the biggest problem--is Medicaid. In 1981, Medicaid cost $4 billion statewide. Today, this program costs New Yorkers $14 billion, accounting for over 10% of all state and local government spending.

Little of this enormous expense is invested in cost control. We should be spending more on primary physician care (so that people get treatment before their conditions require hospitalization), and less on long-term care. But instead of restructuring the program, Albany has opted for a quick fix: freeze Medicaid reimbursement rates, and allow hospitals to recoup their Medicaid costs by tacking on charges to Blue Cross/Blue Shield and employers' self-insured plans.

In effect, Albany forces private employers to help balance the state budget. The employers, in turn, have asked employees to bear a larger share of health care costs. Despite all this cost shifting, New York's Medicaid budget is still out of control. In fiscal years 1990 and 1991, for example, total program costs rose by 17.9% and 16.5%, respectively. Inpatient hospital costs rose still faster, up by 25.6% in 1990 and 23.8% in 1991.

New York has also dramatically expanded its regulatory reach under the Cuomo administration, as evidenced by the enormous growth in agencies such as the Department of Environmental Conservation. Virtually no effort is made to weigh the unseen economic costs of state regulations against their reputed benefits.

The regulatory culture also stymies budget cutting. New York State's nursing homes and hospitals, for example, are saddled with mandated, requirements in record keeping, staffing, nursing services, and patients rights, that go well beyond federal standards. A system desperately in need of renovation is told where to put medicine cabinets and the length of side rails on beds. Ultimately such micro-management works against the interests of those it was designed to aid. A classic example, notes Mr. Reinfurt, is what we've managed to do--or not do--with Life Care Communities for the elderly. State regulations have prevented even one of the planned communities for seniors from opening in New York State. Connecticut and Pennsylvania have consequently reaped a windfall of well-to-do New Yorkers.

However the budget crisis evolves, there are things that can be done. A serious effort to help business would enact reforms in workers compensation programs, product liability laws, and in New York's heavy-handed approach to implementing the Clean Air Act. The state should reduce its estate tax, which is one of the factors that induces many company presidents to move their operations to other states.

New York's drop below 1 million manufacturing jobs should be taken as an alarming sign of New York's problems. Ed Reinfurt may have the solutions.

11 Interview: E.S. Savas

This interview with Steve Savas is based on Ed Rubenstein's notes--it is not a transcript.

PRIVATIZATION

HL: You know about the work of James Buchanan. The natural inclination of government is to grow because the vested interests that benefit from such growth are much better organized than the citizenry at large. Given this political fact of life, how do you develop a constituency for privatization?

SS: Privatization has occurred even in Albania - the People's Republic of New York lags behind.

HL: Yes, 26 states have developed plans to privatize roads. How to do it here?

SS: I don't think that grand ideas sell in the political arena. The most effective strategy is small or micro. Take Ed Rendell, the Mayor of Philadelphia--a Democrat, by the way. He pointed out how much public employees are paid, how many days they actually work (202/year?), how many perks they had, including days off--not even mentioning the tendency of some municipal workers to knock off after a few hours on the job. This polarized the employees, but the public got mad and he was able to assemble support. In New York, McKinsey & Co. has documented the absurdly high hourly wage paid to Transit Authority (TA) employees. Journalist Maureen Connolly followed a garbage truck, at my suggestion--it started at 7:20 instead of 7:00, after a coffee break, and ended the workday at 11 a.m. You can show many examples of mismanagement and mal-practice. This makes people mad.

HL: Examples, please, of government operations which can be privatized.

SS: Solid waste collection and disposal; street sweeping; WNYC; bus operations; hospitals; parks maintenance; school and hospital meal services; vehicle fleet maintenance; building maintenance; and wastewater treatment. The airports--Port Authority management resists this, even though Kennedy Airport is losing market share. The PA spent a lot of money at JFK to build a useless tunnel. Britain has privatized major airports--Gatwick--and in this country Lockheed has expressed interest in buying Los Angeles International.

There is no reason why OTB, offtrack betting, can't be run by a private company. The bookies laugh at it--a bookie that is losing money!

ER: OTB, like Kennedy airport, is probably losing market share in the New York City area. That is, the illegal bookies are getting an even larger share of the betting dollar.

SS: More money is squandered doing the wrong thing well than in doing the right thing poorly. Economists would call this suboptimal behavior--doing things well that shouldn't be done at all.

HL: Where has privatization caught on?

SS: Look at what Mayor Steve Goldsmith has done in Indianapolis, or Mayor Daley in Chicago.

HL: I know Goldsmith. You are careful to point out that "privatization" really means competition between the private and public spheres. In Arizona, the public sector eventually won a contract by coming in lower than the private bidders. Are there any other examples of this?

SS: Look at Newark--they did a great job 20 years ago when Gibson was mayor, and now under Sharpe James. Speak to Al Zach their chief engineer and Frank Sudol, his deputy. The city went from 1,700 to 600 employees in one area, delivering better service. They have good literature to backup their privatization initiative.

HL: I was on a panel discussion with Sharpe James and was amazed that he and I shared the same views on privatization.

SS: Another "micro" example that you should point out is that federal transportation funding (mass transit monies), sent to New York State, has been used exclusively for higher wages and benefits, not for increased infrastructure. There have been no new rail lines built with this money. It wasn't earmarked for personnel, but that's where the money was spent.

New York's highly regulated transportation industry has five levels of taxi service--yellow, black cars, gypsies, liveries, and route vans. The vans provide a decent service for $1.00; city buses cost about $4.00 per ride. Bus riders usually earn less than the bus drivers. But when I mention this to people at the city TA, the response is "Yes, the vans are stealing our riders." That's the kind of answer I used to hear in Brezhnev's Russia, which I visited numerous times...

ER: Is New York State a special case when it comes to privatization?

SS: Everyone is scared in New York because of the unions. But when I spoke to Cuomo he was very charming and said he supported privatization.

HL: I think he was saying that for your benefit.

SS: I'm not so sure. I think the political calculus has changed. It used to be that to get elected in this state you put more people on the payroll. Now the successful politicians are the ones who keep services high and costs low.

HL: I see no evidence that this Governor is interested in reducing the state's payroll or costs. Take the three ski resorts operated by the state. There is no reason why a state--this state or any other--must operate ski resorts. The users are primarily high income "yuppie" types, so there is no egalitarian goal served by putting money into these things. When I asked the Governor about this he cited an obscure law from the State Constitution that requires the state to maintain ski trails. It dates from the days when skiing was the only mode of winter transportation in the mountains, and yet he used it to defend a frivolous expense.

SS: It is difficult to privatize things in New York City. We privatized street light maintenance to eight contractors, but it drifted back to just one. Something was going on--bid-rigging or collusion.

HL: It's hard to establish a privatization constituency with so many municipal employees. New York City has 540 municipal employees per 10,000 in the population. Multiply that by three, to take a family into account. Add in the beneficiaries and you almost have a majority either working for the city or on the dole.

SS: But there is a lot of private resentment--you can't just multiply.

HL: What does it take to create a pro-privatization consensus? A crisis?

SS: We are close to a precipice. Philadelphia was bankrupt--over the precipice. And Ed Rendell, a Democrat, ran TV ads touting privatization, and he, of course, was elected. Cities die slowly--look at Athens, Rome.

Blacks are more in favor of school vouchers than the public at large. Polly Williams in Milwaukee has mobilized black voters for vouchers. School choice, via vouchers and charter schools, is the last hope for New York City's education system.

America Works, a private company, finds jobs for welfare recipients. This can be greatly expanded. Use the private sector for many social services, but through competition.

HL: A major problem is that minorities hold a disproportionate share of city jobs, and they fear loss of jobs through privatization.

SS: My research shows that when you cut back on city jobs--privatize-- minority workers come out no worse. By and large state and local regulations hurt small business and many of those small businesses are minority owned. These regulations have also led to a growing underground economy with immigrants working off the books. The regulations drove them underground. Peter Guttman was the first to write about the underground economy.

Commentary: ER

Steve Savas has spent his entire career showing governments how to do more with less. The key, according to Savas, is privatization-- allowing private firms to compete against government agencies. Savings from competitive contracting have traditionally averaged between 25 to 30 percent.

A decade ago, privatization was an academic abstraction. Liberal politicians dismissed "contracting out," "public asset sales," and "school choice" as schemes concocted by right-wing ideologues. Public employee unions feared layoffs, lower wages, and a rising non-union workforce. The "P-word" buzzed loudly in certain think tanks, but was swatted down everywhere else.

Today, more than 200 types of government services have been opened up to private providers. Nearly one-third of all American cities contract or franchise private firms to collect solid waste; private toll-roads have been built in Virginia and California, and have been authorized in Arizona, and Florida; in several states entire state hospital systems have been privatized.

Mass transit is provided by private companies in more than thirty major cities in the United States. Newark, New Jersey started privatizing its municipal bus lines more than a decade ago. When this program started, the private lines cost 21% less than the city-run lines. Over time, the pressures of competition forced the city workforce to become more efficient, and the gap narrowed to only to 9%. Bus user surveys showed no difference in the quality of service between the private and municipal lines. Meanwhile, in New York City, small unsubsidized van owners make money charging passengers $1, while city buses lose money at $1.25 per passenger.

Social services have been in the forefront of the privatization movement. Many state and local governments have contracted with privately run mental retardation facilities, day care centers, and child support enforcement offices. America Works, a private contractor, teaches welfare recipients how to look for jobs in New York State. Some counties have hired private firms to administer their AFDC and medicaid caseloads, cutting administrative costs as well as payment error rates.

More than thirty state prisons are currently managed and maintained by private companies. In addition to normal security, these companies provide health care, drug treatment programs, education and vocational training. Private prisons cost significantly less to run per inmate, and the conditions are usually better than they were when the same facilities were run by the government.

The ideal approach is to let private firms and public agencies compete against each other. If the government agency comes in with the low bid, then privatization would essentially only preserve the status quo. In Phoenix, for example, the city sanitation department underbid private carters on certain privatized routes.

In fact, it is misleading to think of contracting out in terms of public versus private. It is really a case of monopoly versus competition--with the public sector one of the competitors. Nor is competition between the public and private sectors anti-union: private sector unions can be expected to supplant public sector unions. Neither is it anti-worker, for by matching the rate of privatization to the normal attrition rate, no worker need be laid off. Public employees are often offered jobs in the newly privatized entities.

In 1992 Steve Savas directed the Lauder Commission's study on privatization. The final report tallied the potential savings: $10 billion per year in operating expenses, plus a one-time $3 billion in sales tax receipts, by contracting out, competition, and selling public assets in New York State. A June 1993 report by the New York City Partnership Privatization Task Force, *Putting People First: Making New York Work Through Privatization and Competition*, identified citywide savings of nearly $16 billion over ten years.

Unfortunately, New York is stuck in the study phase. We lag behind the nation in implementing privatization, and it shows. Our governments are among the least efficient in the nation. In 1990, state and local taxes per capita in New York were 62% higher than the national average. Per capita spending by the state was 50% higher, leading seven similar states--Massachusetts, New Jersey, California, Michigan, Illinois, Ohio, and Pennsylvania.

But higher "prices" have not bought higher service levels or quality:
- New York spent $7,663 per student in 1989--65% more than the national average, yet ranked 42nd in average SAT scores and had the lowest graduation rate of any large state. Even Mississippi, with child poverty rates nearly double those of New York, had a higher rate.
- New York employed one highway worker per each 6.2 miles of

highway, or twice as many workers per mile as the national average, yet the percent of deficient bridges in New York is twice the average.
- In 1990 California served 1.3 million more Medicaid recipients than New York, offered more optional services, but spent $5.3 billion less on Medicaid than New York.
The high cost of government in New York State is often blamed on lax management and greedy labor unions. Yet public sector managers everywhere are rewarded for higher budgets and larger staffs; and labor unions always put the interests of their members first. Our problem stems from a government monopoly in which efficiency incentives do not exist. Privatization might be the solution.

12 Interview: Henry Stern

HL: Our basic concern is state government, and state affairs, so you can start anywhere.

HS: My focus for thirty two years, my work for the City of New York, and now as president of a city-wide civic organization is to observe the state as basically an institution that provides funds for the city, collects taxes and revenue. The operations of state government are relatively limited within the City of New York to the police, fire, sanitation, arts, health and human resources. The state provides health services, and workers' compensation, but it isn't the presence that city government is, which is why the governor is less visible than the mayor. If anything happens, if there's an emergency, a fire, someone is shot, a flood, the mayor is expected to be on the scene. Not the governor, who is remote, a kind of viceroy. So, if you ask what state policy can be changed, I don't think most New York City people would have a specific proposal for state policy.

ER: What about social programs where the state really does make policy?

HS: Well, it makes the policy and sets the mandates, as a result of pressures by the state legislature and the executive branch. It has a Democratic Assembly and a Republican Senate. You have constant pressure for new programs. Your basic problem is that it's very hard to determine if these programs work or not. Very often programs turn out to be swindles, one way or the other. And some things which don't have such great intentions turn out to be alright. There's very little certainty in government. Knowing when to do something, when to start nursing homes, for example, or start guaranteeing student loans, may only help others develop "racket" schools. I've always felt the reason for open admissions in the university was not only to educate minorities but to get teaching jobs for the middle class.   It's very difficult for legislators, who run for re-election every two years, who are dependent on contributions and party support and who haven't the insight to evaluate programs, to function freely, unencumbered to outside concerns.

ER: Perhaps it's hard to vote against something that challenges party discipline.

HS: Sure, because its trouble for you, and its going to pass anyway. Whatever is going to pass in the legislature is determined in committee. There are very few issues that come to the floor, where your vote as a legislator will make the difference.   The result is you rely on the leadership.   The same condition prevails in the City Council, unless you have a strong sentiment about something that affects your area.   On that leadership will give you a pass.

ER: So the outcome is already preordained.

HS: Yes. I've observed cases where a borough president will vote against a bill involving his borough and everybody else votes for it. Obviously it passed, but the borough president says, see, I fought it all the way.   There's a lot of inevitable hypocrisy in the political process. Because if you didn't have it, if you are honest about issues, you wouldn't last. You would be thrown out in two years. You wouldn't have the visibility, the unions would turn on you, as well as businesses, and the party. Unless an independent legislator has access to the media, which is usually not the case in New York, he is fairly invisible.

There are 50 assemblymen or more for the City of New York; how is any one assemblyman going to get the attention of newspapers for anything he says or does? That's part of the problem. Who's going to run? What you have to go through to run is humiliating. You don't have intellectuals running as candidates, not that they'd be any better than those in office at the moment. Essentially, community leaders or activists from a neighborhood become the people's candidates. By and large, those elected are decent people, but they're not people with any particular legislative skills, or the ability to pass laws or distinguish between desirable outcomes and undesirable ones, as you see in this particular City Council. You have a speaker, a party leader who expects you to vote a certain way. If you vote differently, you have to account for it. If you offer a reason that suits him, it's okay. If not, he says why should the council pass any of your bills? You get into logrolling. And if you want to accomplish anything in the legislature, which is a cooperative venture, you can only accomplish it when others vote for your bills. And they won't vote for your bills unless you vote for theirs.

HL: Henry, how then do you ever develop a consensus for retrenchment, or is that virtually impossible?

HS: Well, under the fear of running out of money--

HL: So it would have to be a crisis.

HS: Right, an externally imposed crisis. You couldn't possibly get people to shrink government services or government programs voluntarily. The pressures and the demands are to spend more, and do more. That was the irony with Koch. Koch did his best to try to hold down government spending. But his budgets were always increased, not decreased, by the City Council and the Board of Estimate. He was denounced as being unsympathetic and so on. Now, you may say this is terrible; there were fifty thousand jobs created under Koch. But at the time, worse was going on.   He would fight with the Parks Department. When I was Parks Commissioner I would try to get more people in parks, try to get the parks cleaner, and the mayor would hang back and say no. The dynamic of the government is that the greater pressure is always to increase spending. Even from the people who don't want to pay taxes. You don't see people from Suffolk or Nassau saying reduce the budget by thirteen or fifteen percent because they want less assistance for school aid.   Many of the most anti-tax constituencies are also the ones who are supporting new spending. Legislators often say, "If you want this for the suburbs, then give us this for the city." The only thing that varies in this is how many months it takes to divide the spoils. And I don't see how it could it be any other way. You're not the only one with an individual personality. This one's a good guy, this one's a bad guy; you're dealing with a situation where the dynamics compel people to act as representatives of their constituencies. If they fail to do so, the constituencies will select another representative.

HL: But then you have either to artificially create the crisis, or there has to be a real crisis of the kind you had in New York City in 1975.

HS: Right, when you have no money or you're running out of money to pay the bills. What's so interesting here is that when a crisis can be weathered, say by reduction of expenditure, the classic situation is that the unions will balk. If the government has ten percent less to spend next year compared to this year, a department has to take a ten percent cut. There are two possible ways to do it: You can fire ten people or you can reduce everyone's wages ten percent. Clearly, the right thing in the public interest is to reduce everyone's wages ten percent, so that you keep more people going to work and they don't have to go on unemployment. But no union and no labor leader will support that proposal, because as a union leader you have to run for re-election. I have a choice: I can have 90 happy members or 100 unhappy members. If I have 100 unhappy members they will throw me out; 90 happy members would vote me in. So even though I may personally agree with you that the better thing to do is take a ten percent cut, it's incompatible with my survival as head of this union.

ER: It also creates a bad precedent if you're a union leader.

HS: Absolutely.

HL: Then matters like bond ratings are irrelevant from a government standpoint unless, in fact, it becomes impossible for you to sustain spending. What you're talking about is the inevitable crowding out of private capital. You're simply saying, we're going to increase spending each year, by some indeterminate factor.

HS: Well, I don't see any political forces that would compel increased spending. It's not a choice between the poor or the middle class. The middle class in the suburbs want heavily subsidized school aid, and the poor want welfare assistance. Everybody has a stake, of one kind or other, in state spending.

ER: So a tax revolt doesn't hold much chance of succeeding.

HL: The point, which is an interesting one, is those people who may be involved in the tax revolt still like to get their goodies from government. And that is particularly true in Nassau and Suffolk counties where you have the two largest anti-tax groups in New York State and yet all of them are receiving the benefits of aid for education.

HS: It's a very heavy bias, too, a disproportionate bias. I don't see how people could vote for someone in the executive branch as an anti-tax candidate with the economy running down and with the relative competitive position of the state deteriorating and with the state being the point of entry to the United States for poor immigrants with enormous social problems.

HL: The staggering figure of more than one million people on welfare in New York City is an interesting symbol.

HS: Yuppies on welfare too. People who are not really poor, who didn't come to the city to get welfare. It's interesting that when the system expands, you get a lot of people on welfare who aren't beating the system, who are legitimate examples. Unless there's a jobs program I don't see the welfare system will change. It's a terrible thing not to have a job, not to be able to get a job. You have no meaning as a person. It's overwhelming, and I somehow think that at some level government has to ultimately be the provider of jobs.

ER: I don't think there's been any jobs program that's been a success, either federal or state.

HS: But in the 1930s...

ER: WPA?

HS: WPA was a success. My uncle worked in that.

HL: Not in securing real jobs, Henry.

HS: So they're not real jobs. But at least they give people something to do and they do public works.

HL: Tell me, if Clinton wins, let's assume for a second that he does, how do you think it will affect New York City and New York State?

HS: There will be a much more favorable attitude on the part of the federal government for New York City and New York State. I think Clinton would see New York as an important part of his electoral majority, his political strength.

HL: How would that favorable attitude be manifested? Would it mean more federal assistance, more federal sharing?

HS: Yes, in all the little ways. If Clinton wins there won't be so much carping. If you have the reverse, you'll have Mayor Dinkins blaming the Federal government for all his troubles. And then you'll have the feds blame the city for mismanagement. They're both wrong. After twelve years of blaming the cities, the results are terrible.

HL: Let me make the argument about New York that you've undoubtedly heard, that would be the conservative argument. Why should the federal government be concerned with the problems of the city when the city has created its own problems with a superfluous socialistic bureaucracy, more people employed in the public sector (per ten thousand) than almost any other place in the world, why should the federal government be interested in the city when the city contributes to its own problems with rent control and other forms of government intervention?

HS: There is validity to those conditions. On the other hand, there are 7 million people who live here and there are new people coming in every week, every month, from a different country and if the policies were different we would still have enormous problems. If there were no rent control there would still be homeless people. Rent control has little to do with homelessness.

HL: According to Bill Tucker, there is some relationship.

HS: The problem, the very important problem, is mental health. We have so many people who have varying degrees of impairment. The other day, I saw two or three people having inappropriate conversations on the subway acting crazy. In New York we get used to it. We have no way of dealing with people who are impaired, we don't know what to do with them. The government doesn't want to reinstitutionalize them.

HL: Why not?

HS: Well, because some days the courts won't let you; Ed Koch tried. And then there are people who drift between being well and being ill. There's a whole twilight world out there where people are moderately impaired.

ER: But do you really think this problem is worse now than it was 25 years ago?

HS: It's more visible.

ER: But its not inherently worse.

HS: Oh, I think so--

ER: Why should there be more mental illness today than then?

HS: Probably because of drugs, the breakup of the nuclear family. Because of the popular culture of sex and violence, because there's less sense of responsibility toward others, toward family members. I think there's far more crazy people than there were when I was kid.

ER: But they weren't allowed to loiter on the streets.

HL: Vagrancy laws were always enforced. I knew crazy people in my neighborhood in Brooklyn and the cops would say, I'm sorry, you're not allowed to be on the streets. When the Democratic convention was held in New York, they were taken off the streets. So clearly it can be done, as long as you apply enough pressure.

HS: I don't think that the streets should be an open air insane asylum, but when you try to figure out what to do about it you have a lot of problems. I think its one of the things that makes the city very unattractive to people. Due to the benefit policies of the federal government, thousands of dollars a month of cash in disability allowance may be dispersed which a recipient can spend on drugs. That's not the city government, that's a federal policy. There are so many people like that, there are so many impaired people running around who are increasingly threatening to others, that people don't

want to live here. What now happens is that these social factors have
a sufficient impact on the quality of life to make people choose to live
elsewhere. It's like the pond that putrefies, it goes dead. Of course it's
not only here; I read in the paper today that an MIT student was slain
in Cambridge, and a Yale student was killed. I think you're getting
more of that with the breakdown in social norms. That's not a function
of tax policy.

ER: It certainly differentiates the present crisis from the one in 1975.

HS: Yes. It is a social crisis as well as an economic crisis. But
nobody can deal with a social crisis. Part of the problem of a social
crisis is you run into the realm of political correctness. Anything you
might do will seem sexist, racist or homophobic. On the other hand, I
haven't seen anybody come up with proposals that make sense. The
proposals that are made are always about greater spending. There was
a hearing in the City Council on Beacon schools, keeping schools open
16 hours a day so people would have a place to go. Seemed very
sensible, if you have no home, live in a poor neighborhood, want to
have some shelter in the city and don't want to get beaten up. But it
was evaluated solely as a spending bill.

HL: Isn't there a way to privatize some services?

HS: Yes, but another bill that was put before the City Council today
in a hearing, would make it practically impossible to privatize anything.

HL: That's to protect municipal unions.

HS: I call it the Public Employee Protection Act. Its got 19 co-
sponsors in City Council and all these people are voting for union
support.

HL: So then a productivity standard within government, as Osborne of
Reinventing Government suggests, is virtually impossible in New York.

HS: Well, what's interesting is that even the Dinkins administration
would take a favorable attitude on this matter. Keep in mind, the
unions endorse candidates; people come to the unions for City Council

candidates, for money. Why can't the unions ask for something since they can't ask for money. Two bills came up in City Council just this morning. One is a proposal to spend more on the schools, the other is a proposal to prevent privatization. So you don't see anything going further, you only see them talking about the issues that you present.

ER: Can Dinkins point to a reduction in the city's head count?

HS: He's taking points for a reduction in head counts. Except the police, of course. The police, who he's really helped, are the least grateful. So there's the irony of it.

HL: You paint a very interesting scenario, Henry, but one that I must tell you is somewhat depressing.

HS: So I think the issues have to be competence and the ability to administer, and let me generalize about moderation in government. I don't see the social arguments winning, I don't see, with the media as progressive as it is, Dan Quayle winning the social arguments.

HL: Well I think that here again, Henry, it's easy to attack the messenger rather than the message. The message that he conveyed about Murphy Brown is perfectly sensible. Look, this is a cavalier decision made on tv where a woman quite obviously of the middle class decides to have a child out of wedlock. For the rest of the nation this is catastrophic; illegitimacy is having a baneful effect on the economy, is having a baneful effect on our social lives, its destroying our cities, and we should realize that. We should certainly not treat this in a cavalier fashion.

HS: It would seem to me that for a person like Murphy Brown, who clearly is able to support herself, to support the child, that is not unreasonable for her.

HL: Oh, it's certainly not Henry. But it's not the Murphy Browns that concern me. If I were Mick Jagger having kids out of wedlock, I say what the hell, Mick Jagger can support ten families, he can have 20 kids out of wedlock. It's this kid on the streets, this black kid, who defines his machismo by making babies and who has ten kids out of wedlock and doesn't take care of them. That's the kind of family that

I think is having such a corrosive effect on family.

HS: As far as what you can do about the city's liability: obviously you can't have claims against the city adjudicated by juries, it has to be the same way at the state level--you have to have the support of the courts. But you never would get that because the legislature is full of lawyers. New York is in a pre-revolutionary situation. Privilege is very vested in certain categories of people: employees, pensioners, welfare recipients. People who get checks from the City of New York are as many as the people who write checks to the City of New York. And it is people who write the checks who leave. So you have a fundamental imbalance there, that leads me to that wonderful story about the two guys in the country on vacation. One of them runs each morning and the other guy says, why are you running? I'm running, he says, in case a bear attacks. And the other says, you can't run faster than a bear. And the guy says, I don't have to run faster than the bear, I just have to run faster than you. So in that regard there would have to be better places, other places where people could live and locate their business and make their investments other than New York. Life must go on somewhere.

HL: At the moment, where is this advantageous position?

HS: As long as New York is essentially a point of entry for people to the country, Haitians, or whatever they are, this is where you come, this is a cosmopolitan city where you can get some kind of job, if you're willing to work.

ER: You raised another point there. Not whether this city can survive, but should we really survive, if there are alternatives elsewhere. The people who do care are the ones who have the vested interest in the situation--the real estate industry and the utilities. I've always thought of them as the two captives of the city. If you have real estate in New York, you can't move into New Jersey, and if you hook the steam pipes into the city you can't hook that anyplace either.

HS: Yeah, what you can do is sell your real estate in New York. Many real estate companies are building outside New York, and have been doing so for some years.

HL: Well, you can't build in New York.

HS: Right. And when you try a project like Riverside South, neighborhood people are screaming against it. On top of everything else, nobody wants to build. I think if things change, if you could make money building, then those pressures would abate. But there's certainly a "No Build" mentality in this town. In some areas, even clean six story houses are highly objectionable. People say they want density, but there's the old saying that nobody hates the next high rise like the last high rise. Especially if it blocks your view. So you have all those obstacles. But usually when there's development money and you want to do something you can create jobs, the pressures to build can overcome many obstacles. Now there's no pressure to build and nobody wants to build.

HL: It's hard to overcome the detractors.

HS: That's why the Mayor's Capital Program is, to my mind, very poorly conceived. Because he wants to spend hundreds of millions of dollars building the police academy in the Bronx. He wants to spend more millions fixing the courts. And all of it is basically a structure to serve the bureaucracy, to serve the employees. However the city is not doing the right economic things to make the city more competitive.

ER: There is a big factor in city development and that's tax abatement.

HL: And that is entirely arbitrary. There's nothing systematic; it's entirely political.

HS: There are people who are using tax abatement now for their own advantage. It's a problem. It's a whole network of interlocking interests that promote resentment. Some would say, why give abatements to rich guys when the large majority of people want opportunities of their own. Why should anyone be trusted to assist the poor in the inner cities when the record is so bad.

HL: You may supplant the white leadership in the bureaucracy but if you lose that tax base, who's going to pay the bills for the bureaucracy? It's a kind of naivete.

HS: Yes. But what's interesting is that Dinkins has resisted layoffs as much as he can. He certainly hasn't been able to make changes and services have declined. Now, when you're looking for an opening in this political field, concerned with how you get something which is better than what you have, then I think the hope is voters who seek change. Some of the same seesaw principle that helped Clinton in '92. It might help a republican in '94.

Commentary: HL

Standing astride Plato's *Republic*, Henry Stern asks yet again if a democratic republic is governable. As he notes in claims which are unencumbered by pretense, there is an inexorable pressure for ever greater expenditures, notwithstanding a dispassionate assessment of available resources. As he notes, if you want to accomplish anything in the state legislature, you must support the legislation of others so they will support yours. Logrolling is in the best tradition of democracy. As a consequence, in his judgment, the essential dynamic in government is to increase spending even if this practice erodes the tax base and crowds out private capital.

The road to fiscal responsibility is paved with an externally imposed crisis. Presumably, the fiscal crisis of 1977 in New York City was prompted by the unwillingness of the banks to underwrite the city's debt. At that point, the need for fiscal restraint was overwhelming. Yet a crisis is largely in the eye of the beholder: municipal union leaders are often reluctant to admit that a crisis exists which warrants a ten percent reduction in the state- supported workforce. And even middle class residents want continued government subsidies for commuter rail systems and suburban schools. With everyone feeding at the public trough in one form or another it is most difficult to create a political consensus for decreased spending even with the specter of fiscal disaster on the near horizon.

As Henry Stern notes, reaching a voluntary threshold for responsible but reduced government activity in the face of mounting problems borne of high immigration, so-called homelessness, and high unemployment, is a will-of-the-wisp idea. Or is it? There is little doubt that many people rely on government to find answers to what ails us. The "nanny" state in all its manifestations is present in New York.

However, it is always easy but not always correct to assume that what people are accustomed to is what they must have. Leadership, in my judgment, is based on the proposition that the people, or 50 percent plus one, can be persuaded to change course. Free ridership - or the belief that someone else will pay for the things you want - is a condition manifest in outworn Marxist suppositions. There isn't a free lunch, even though many New Yorkers have been led to believe that breakfast, lunch and dinner are free. The edifice of state is crumbling, and not because New York cannot raise revenue. It can and does. In 1993, tax revenues in New York surpassed $36 billion. The problem is an insatiable appetite for spending that isn't satisfied by revenue and, even after well advertised draconian measures, is still two and a half times the rate of inflation.

What New York seemingly craves, and what Henry Stern's astute analysis calls for, is old fashioned leadership. An agenda based on reduced state expenditures explained as the condition necessary to attract private capital could be the framework for a campaign and could serve as a mandate for reform. Politics may be the art of the possible, but the seemingly intractable problems of yesterday can become the opportunities of tomorrow in deft hands. Moreover, although Mr. Stern neglects to mention it, the governor has line item veto and impoundment power which allow him to cut the budget unilaterally. Here, the will to lead has its natural expression in a power granted the governor and denied the president. The only constraint on gubernatorial power in this regard is restoring funds that have been cut by either of the houses of state government.

Henry Stern's experience and background in municipal affairs has given him insights into the deep-rooted privileges which groups can arrogate for themselves. But however these special favors and conditions evolve, there is a market mechanism of a kind that is also at work: people can vote with their feet and do. In the decade of the 1980's about 1.5 million New Yorkers left this state for the greener pastures of Florida, Nevada, Texas and even contiguous states - states that haven't any personal income tax at all or lower rates. In the 1990's so far, more than 500,000 people have left the state. Those departing are invariably people with financial options. The poor and welfare recipients are generally not on the departure list.

The consequence of this migration is that if New York wants to keep its productive citizens, the ones who pay the bills, then it will have to compete with other states. It will have to create an environment congenial to business and capable of creating jobs. It will have to introduce a competitive tax rate and it will be forced into the position of controlling, if not curtailing, expenditures to which many New Yorkers are accustomed. In short, Henry Stern has defined the problem but not the necessary steps leading to solvency and state survival.

Can a politician run on a Jeffersonian stance that government is best which rules least? It is an arguable proposition that has not been tested. It may be hard to wean people off welfare and wean the middle class from its stake in government benefits. However, "tough love" in the present climate may produce understanding and a more productive state economy than we have known in the last two decades.

13 Interview: William Stern

HL: Let's start by talking about the role of the Urban Development Commission (UDC) in state government. In recent years its role seems to have changed from that of a construction agency to a unit that bails out the Governor when he runs into a budget problem.

WS: That bail-out use of the UDC began in the Carey administration. The UDC was originally formed to build public housing after the Martin Luther King riots. UDC then was given enormous powers to float bonds and do sales lease-backs, selling properties and leasing them back, or buying something and leasing it back. It could override local zoning laws, override local taxation, override sales taxes. So the UDC is an authority with enormous power. Comes the threat of the close of Radio City in the Carey administration, the Carey administration starts to use those powers for something other than low-income public housing.

The Cuomo administration has just run with the same ball. UDC was used as a vehicle to build prisons when the prison bond issue was voted down. The UDC under Governor Carey was used to underwrite the Javits convention center. People don't realize the center was financed by bonds issued by the Triborough Bridge and Tunnel Authority. They used the TBTA credit to raise money for the convention center even though it had nothing to do with TBTA business. UDC has the power to form subsidiary authorities; Battery Park City is one. Often the director of these authorities gets appointed by the legislature as well as the governor.

If you did an organization chart of the convention center project, which overran its budget, you would not be able to find out who was in charge. So you could not only disguise financing mechanisms, but also authority, accountability. The various state authorities have been turned into financial opportunities for political insiders, Wall Street public finance departments and the Governor's cronies who get lucrative patronage jobs. Because authorities have a higher salary structure, the idea was that they could attract top talent. But they don't. What they do, is enable the Governor to fill a few lucrative patronage jobs, and also enable him to use the authority's financial power to artfully dance around the states' requirement for a balanced budget. That is the authority's true power. So what you have is a political insider racket in which a large number of people participate. Sometimes I think that's almost what elections are about here: who's going to be the top of the pyramid in this racket. Republicans, Democrats, liberals, conservatives - these people have no ideology. It's a spoils system that would probably make Boss Tweed a piker.

ER: When I interviewed you last year you described it as a system for the upward distribution of income.

WS: Yes. The redistribution is from ordinary people to political insiders, the *nomenclatura*. So many people are included in one way or another, including people in the press, that it's a dirty little secret of New York politics and government. It's so discouraging in a way because it kind of makes political dialogue -- liberal/conservative views on public policy issues -- an amusement park that political tourists visit. It's either an act that people put on during the campaign, like I'm the liberal, you're the conservative, let's play that role on the stage, and then, after the election, we'll go back to the real work, which is making money. The public is really interested in ideas, so they think the election is about issues, when it's really about control of the rackets. I came away, unfortunately, not cynical, but very depressed about public service.

HL: Is there any way of reforming the system? Or is it just a hopelessly insidious web that can not be changed?

WS: I think it's fellows like you who would know more about reforming it. I'd like to see the commercial reality of it discussed more. Maybe that's the beginning of the reform.

HL: I think you brought it to my attention - the Wayne Barrett piece in the *Village Voice* about Cuomo and his relationship to UDC and other authorities.

WS: Yes, Wayne is a great investigative reporter who writes about the rackets. Many of his stories are published but unfortunately just die. The commercial maneuvering is what we're calling government and this reality is being disguised.

When I left government and travelled to Eastern Europe I had it described to me clearly there. I talked to people who were very familiar with Communist systems all through Eastern Europe. They described the reality of the Communist system, but wouldn't dignify the government officials by calling them Marxists or Communists. They were very clear in calling them scammers, racketeers. They made it very clear that the government officials were racketeers using Marxist rhetoric to disguise their true purpose. The ideology was a disguise for the racketeering.

I noticed a similar analysis in the Presidential election, when Ross Perot talked about the "public servants" who left their jobs in the White House for $300,000 a year jobs working for foreign countries on trade agreements. It's known all over that the way to deal with the United States in trade negotiations is to tap dance and then hire the public servant you negotiated with. Perot used it for his own advantage. He hired them. He's probably angry because he had to hire them.

ER: It's systemic corruption.

WS: Yes, it's really a manifestation of the welfare state mentality. Going to work in a campaign is much better than going to college, because if your candidate wins, you're on your way. We could list the names of many people who have leveraged political power into big bucks. What they're selling is the fact that they know a lot of political insiders. They're not selling legal skills, engineering skills, managerial skills.

ER: Is it any different now than it ever was? Is it the nature of democracy?

WS: No. It's not so different now. I think all sin goes back a long time. I think what happened was that we expanded it - we blew up the government. With the welfare state, we expanded the government and made the whole racket bigger. It's like murder. We all know there are more murders going on in New York than ever, but I imagine we could go back to the very early days in New York and find a murder or two. Similarly, the insider racket is larger now than ever, but it always existed.

HL: So you regard partisanship as a kind of silly notion. It doesn't make any difference if they are Democrats or Republicans, liberals or conservatives, they're all getting a handout and they're all in the game.

WS: They're all in the game, they're all in the *nomenclatura*. Partisanship would be important if we could straighten out the system. But this is like an albatross, making a joke out of the so called political process. I was involved for eight years, four years full time, in one of the most unsatisfactory experiences of my life. I started out thinking that it would be a very satisfactory and rewarding experience. It's sad, I think it offends a lot of people.

HL: Where is the muckraker? After all, we live in a society where journalists are interested in precisely this kind of story. But where is the muckraker who's writing this story about the inside game of government?

WS: Well, you see it in the *Village Voice*, and you see it in the Gannett chain of newspapers, but it's not systematically exposed in the major league media. My opinion is that often, they're part of it. To me it's not irrational that so many real estate developers want to buy publications. If you're in a government regulated business you can best influence the process by owning a paper. That's far more effective than contributing to a political campaign.

If I were a real estate developer in New York City it would be very logical to buy a newspaper as an adjunct to my real estate business. I think the newspapers in New York routinely involve themselves in real estate power-brokering. On the 42nd Street Redevelopment project, which I ran for the state, I'm sorry to say the developers spent as much time at the *New York Times* as they did with me.

I look upon New York now as a kind of United States of Ireland. The young people in Ireland live in a system that creates no jobs. They simply emigrate. The tradition of emigration is strong -- both here and in Ireland. So the culture is not reform-minded, because the young who are educated, who would be the ones to naturally lead reform, simply leave. New York's economy has been fading since 1950, a trend disguised by the resurgence of financial services in the 1980s. Basically we're in decline as a state, and we're losing lots of people. We're losing the affluent elderly and the educated young. What do we have? One-third less congressional representation than we did in 1950; I think it's 43 versus 31. So we have had a huge loss. I've often thought New York needed a reformer like Gorbachev-an insider to decide that it's not working.

HL: Is it not working because the general conditions are uncongenial for business activity, or is it the crime on the streets, or is it because the tax structure militates against it? Or is it everything?

WS: I wouldn't establish a priority for what's wrong. It's a very, very oppressive climate for business growth because of the legal taxes and the illegal corruption taxes. The cost of doing business here drowns the economy. Economically we're not growing, but fading, and I think it's because our political culture is degenerate and unable to reform itself. If you talk to people who have spent time in the political culture you'll find many have arrived at pretty much the same conclusion. I run into people all the time who believe that we have a corrupt political culture.

HL: Would a crisis precipitate this change? A bond default?

WS: Yes. But that was a 1970s crisis. I don't see any crisis like that now. I see erosion.

HL: The erosion occurs incrementally, therefore it's hard to conceive of it as a crisis. These departures from New York have been going on for a long time. We lost 300,000 people during the 1980s but I didn't hear anyone say that this loss of population base is a crisis. After all, the people who are leaving are those who have tax dollars to take with them. It's not the poor, the indigent or the welfare recipients who leave the state.

WS: Unless the decay accelerates like an avalanche, I don't see a conventional crisis.

HL: The ones who remain here want to derive something from the system. There are goodies there for them. But you don't have to be a rocket scientist to see the erosion of the goodies. New York can't continue to self-destruct.

WS: You can certainly hear real estate developers who participated in the system, and often used it for their benefit, say they're concerned. Because in the end, you can't be sure of being the individual who gets the tax breaks. In the system we had in the 1980s, certain people were designated to pay less in taxes than other people. They played the game of being the last person the alligator eats, and now they're looking into the jaws of the alligator. There is concern. The businessman who thought he was politically connected and wired, and got special tax breaks for his building, now realizes that the value of the building is decreasing rapidly.

ER: I think the Clinton administration, unfortunately, is regarded as the savior for a lot of these people.

WS: They think Clinton will use federal dollars to bail out New York. I don't think he can do that. President Carter used to talk about federalizing welfare, and then somebody figured out that it would add about $30 billion to the budget at that time. That was a big issue, and Senator Moynihan used to talk about it. But they didn't do it then and are not going to do that now. In the end, there is no political savior who's going to throw us a life raft. We've done it to ourselves, we New Yorkers, and either we get out of it ourselves, or we continue to decline. Sometimes I look at it as inevitable decline. We can certainly afford to live elsewhere. But if you were born and raised in New York and you have an attachment to New York, the problem is the next generation. They weren't raised with this kind of neighborhood attachment. Maybe these immigrant groups will step forward and say, look, we want a place for the future. Or maybe we'll have a Gorbachev emerging among the *nomenclatura* saying we're declining here, and we've got to change. I've often thought the *New York Times* would wake up one morning and see the error of their ways. It's not on the horizon yet, and it's certainly not going to be done by Republicans unless there's a total reform of the Republican party. I often hope the Republicans lose the state senate so that they have no political power, no goodies to give out. Then you might have something similar to the Republicans in the assembly: an idea group. In a sense, that's what happened to the national Republican party after Watergate. If you don't have power then you're left with the true believers.

In a way, it's similar to what happens with a religion in a society of religious repression like eastern Europe. When the communists first took over it could cost you your life to be a believer in any of the major religions. Later, the communists moderated and said that you simply couldn't get ahead in life, you couldn't go to the right school. So they were left, all the major religions there, with actual believers. Those believers controlled their religions and the religions became much more powerful and meaningful. To be Jewish in the Soviet Union you had to really believe in Judaism. Otherwise you just sort of melted into the culture. Out of true Jewish believers came Sharansky, and a kind of powerful "next year in Jerusalem" kind of feeling.

So I think that in a lesser way, that can happen in a political party. If the Republicans lost the state senate, and the leadership gang disappeared, then you'd be left with people who believed in political principles and ideas, and it could be something you would rally around. Probably a really strong Republican Party, small, but growing because it would attract a lot of thinking people. And the people it attracts would be of high character; there'd be nothing materially in it for them. At least until they get power and the process starts all over again.

The religions in eastern Europe are very different because they were at the center of the fight against the system.

It's the instinct of New Yorkers to be on the inside. If you're not a believer, you have to be a winner. If you play street corner stick ball, you've got to win the game, it's not how you play the game. In eastern Europe, I heard someone say God loves without manipulation and that's perfect love. In New York we're all from the streets, street smart, maneuvering; we love that part of our culture. But it can be used against us. There is such a thing as right and wrong and a better way of doing things, but soon everyone wants into the racket rather than to reform the racket. That's why it's no surprise that some of our most inside political players start out as reformers. Part of the purpose of reform is that's your gig, you play the reform angle. Another guy is working the ethnic angle, another the racial angle.

HL: The parallels to the Communist world are exactly that. Even there, the reformers are by and large people who simply want to get a piece of the action, who aren't interested necessarily in dismantling the state of communism. That's a minor issue. The ins and outs are what is discussed, who's in, who's out, and who wants to make the deals.

WS: The admiration of success, which can be a very good thing, if it means that you want to develop and try harder, has been used against us. And certainly in New York, because of the history of New York, it has created a really perverse value system. We have to reform our values and change our goals and say that we're not going to place a premium on what we used to place a premium on. When I was at the UDC, I was always amazed at how little power I had. There were so many forces telling me, in one way or another, what to do, that I couldn't keep track of them. So many IOU's, so many interests, that I basically spent my time figuring out who wanted what. I came not to believe in a single economic project, including Battery Park City, and the Convention Center. I think it started with the World Trade Center. Do you really need the government to build luxury apartments? Or Convention Centers? It gets so that nobody believes money going to the schools is going to help the schools because there are a lot of constituencies within the school industry that have to be taken care of.

ER: I heard a story about you, that you wanted to cut UDC's budget and you were called to the carpet for that.

WS: I cut it 15% my first year there, in actual dollars, when I saw how much waste there was in the budget. Because I had committed that mortal sin, I was cut in half. My budget came out of the Governor's office, and the speaker's office cut it in half the next year. They didn't follow through on it, though. They threatened me and made me beg. The number of audits by the state comptroller of UDC were tripled. Actually the speaker took pity on me and was the person who restored the cuts. He thought 50% was a little too harsh a lesson. I was trying to protect the Civil Service employees, give them some kind of tenure so they wouldn't be so susceptible to political pressure. At the time, I thought that would improve the quality of our analysis. The UDC staff would be afraid to give me a real analysis of the economic worth of a project because they were afraid to lose their jobs. So I came up with idea of employment contracts to create tenure, and I was called before the State Investigation Commission. David Trager, who is now a federal judge and was dean of Brooklyn Law School and chairman of the State Investigation Commission at the time, told me that as part of their charter they were empowered to do managerial review. So he made it clear that I wasn't there for any kind of personal corruption. After all, I was working for $1 a year. I said David, people don't think you're a management consultant agency when there are five stories in the *New York Post* about me being called before the SIC. But I, to this day, believe it was a conspiracy to smear my reputation. You know they are looking to smear you. I was put through a wringer. You get stories that you're eccentric, that you believe in things like holistic medicine. I once answered a question saying that holistic medicine was a good concept, and I had the governor's son constantly deriding me, saying, 'well, you know he believes in holistic medicine'. I got a laugh about a year ago when I saw Mario on television talking about we have to be 'holistic' in our approach. Not only was I working for no salary, but it reached the point where I was afraid to ask for reimbursement for a business lunch. I would pay for it out of my own pocket. If you're saying they're sleazy, they're going to try to smear you and then question your stability.

Ken Lipper once said to me, 'in the end you feel like you're playing cowboys and Indians'. You're behind a rock, you lean out and take a few shots, then you're back behind the rock. You don't feel you're making any progress. At the time I had no idea of how widespread it was. Only as time went on did I realize what it was all about. It was striking, at its very core, the commercialization of politics and government.

HL: Anything that could bring about structural change, anything that would slow down the pace of government growth, anything that would lead to reforms where you have less money at your disposal, I think would be desirable.

WS: Absolutely. How do you convince people that it's smart to run an efficient, honest, well organized government-that it's good for the economy, that it's good for New York.

HL: To come back to your analogy of these guys in New York who were manipulators and want to maneuver, wouldn't it be more desirable to have more private capital available instead of the public capital simply driving private capital out of existence?

WS: Sure.

HL: Wouldn't it be more desirable from the point of view of the manipulators-people in the real estate industry and others-to have more private capital at their disposal? Wouldn't it be better for the law firms, or for an investment firm, instead of underwriting New York state bonds, to be involved in a private market? Wouldn't it be more desirable even for the journalists who may be corrupted because of these government contacts, to be writing about what's happening in the private economy?

WS: Take the journalists. They don't realize why there has been a drying up of newspapers. It's because the economy is so poor here. There would be so much more in the way of journalistic jobs and journalistic opportunity if we had a better economy. It's more than just a tax problem or a spending problem. No one truly believes, for example, that these social programs are going to help in any significant way any of our horrific social problems. And no one really believes that even the conservative version of these social programs, things like enterprise zones, vouchers for the schools, vouchers for housing, is going to affect the underclass in any serious way. We should really start discussing what there is about our culture that is creating so many shipwrecked people, that creates so many people who are so devoid of human conscience that they'll abandon their children, they'll maim, they'll behave like a wolf. It's not just a problem of the inner city. It's a problem of the elites I think. It's a problem of example.

HL: It's especially a problem of the elites because in the past they would serve as models to be emulated. But do you emulate the Mick Jaggers of the world who may abandon their families? Or Madonna who is engaged in every kind of sexual perversion one can possibly imagine? I think that the so-called elites have failed us. I think you're right, I don't blame the poor. I blame those who are in a position of establishing models of appropriate behavior.

WS: It's very interesting. We have to be very careful not to worship the market economy. I was very interested in the new Catholic catechism. Pope John Paul talks about modern sins. John Paul has acknowledged capitalism and it's value, but he's very concerned with excessive spending. Elites should not be consuming mindlessly. Elites should be setting an example of investing, saving, moderation. Instead they have given our children the worst possible example in the last twenty years. The less parental strength, the more vulnerable the young person. We all can be very grateful we had parents who really were involved in our lives. The elites in New York are truly horrific.

HL: What you've described you wouldn't describe as capitalism. When Adam Smith wrote about capitalism he said capitalism has to be constrained by moral virtue. He was a moral philosopher after all, he wasn't an economist. So it's a question of capitalism being seen within the constraints of some kind of morality or moral virtue. If it's not, then it's not capitalism-it's what Adam Smith described as anarchism. It's where people simply get for themselves, without any regard at all for the larger culture. The combination of capitalism and selfish behavior leads to deplorable acts. Capitalism must be constrained by moral virtue. That's almost an exact quote from the *Wealth of Nations.*

WS: You're right. I would use another word: materialism. A materialistic view of life has ruined our culture. I find great similarities between New York and Moscow, where they were guided by the materialistic philosophy -- Marxism. Communism is the complete materialistic view of life. We can interpret capitalism as a materialistic view of life, but you're right, capitalism is really an economic system, it's a market.

HL: But there's an element of this that rings very true to me. The words "the pursuit of happiness" in the Declaration of Independence, a phrase that now many regard as an undesirable impulse, was meant in a Jeffersonian sense as virtue. That is, you cannot be happy unless you are also virtuous. Today, the materialistic notion of happiness is equated with having things. If you don't have things, you can't be happy. It's an interesting change that has occurred over the last 200 years, and a rather fascinating one from my point of view. But I think your analysis is correct.

WS: I happen to be a film buff. Get the movies of the 1930s and 40s and see the differences in values that are represented in the movies. Movies are very interesting because they represent a mass culture.

What is the difference between the people I meet now and the people I met as a boy on 125th Street? It's the materialism. Materialistic values were not as important to the people of New York I grew up with. For instance, we had the Italian green grocer, like all New York neighborhoods, at 124 Street & Broadway. The fact that he made a good hero sandwich was very important to him. To be considered a good person, rather than what he owned, was very important. There's been a dramatic change in values, in my lifetime. My mom and dad liked the idea of values. To be moral was a very important value to them.

ER: It's pure capitalism. The guy who makes the best sandwich makes the most money because people come to him. I don't think there's anything wrong with that. There's not necessarily a conflict between doing good and doing well in capitalism. In Communism, you do well by knowing the right people.

WS: Communism says if we reorder the distribution of wealth, if we have an economic system which guarantees each according to his needs etc., etc., then all our problems will go away. It holds that there is no struggle between good and evil, that it will go on regardless of your economic system, that there is no conflict of values. And that's where I mean that capitalism can't be based on materialism alone. We all can be affluent, and behave horrendously. It's a materialistic view of life to say that there aren't other values to life, completely outside material values. I agree with you the good grocer makes the best hero, and should make the most money. But I'm saying, he wanted to make a good hero to be respected, even if he wasn't going to make a lot of money. It was a feeling of service. A feeling that the person who came out to clean the streets after the Department of Sanitation, to finish the job properly, Wally in our neighborhood, was respected. Wally used to come out with his own street sweeper because it delighted him because he was the person responsible for keeping the street clean. It gave him a feeling of status and respect. So all these kinds of values have nothing to do with material values.

Capitalism must be careful. We all can have a million dollars, but can we create a moral society? We have to be careful that the materialism of communism doesn't infect us in the West. In New York you hear it all the time. It cuts into public policy. People say things such as, 'we've got to have enterprise zones'. We have conservatives challenging the bureaucracy of public schools and saying, 'if we have vouchers everything will be all right'. Nothing replaces the love of the parent. Love is not material. Mommy and daddy loving you is the core foundation you need for life and if you don't have that, things can get very difficult -- no matter how much money you have.

There's nothing we can come up with to replace love. It's that which capitalism should guard against-the advancing of material solutions when none are appropriate. We say yes, we want vouchers and competition in the public schools, to give poor parents the same choices as upper middle class parents. A lot of us believe it; everybody who doesn't have a stake in the status quo. All of us have seen what the Catholic schools and the Yeshivas have done. But we've got to remember: nothing replaces mommy and daddy loving you. Why does our society create so little love?

HL: In human history from the Greeks on, and now I probably sound very philosophical, but our discussion is moving in this direction. The Greeks had the great conflict between good and evil. In the Middle Ages, the conflict was between sin and pride, and modernity has the conflict between rich and poor. I think that your analysis is correct, you really need all three. There is the legacy of the past. We still have some sense of good and evil, at least in some sectors of the society. And we still have the conflict between sin and pride in some sectors of the society. But I think modernity, it's not just Marxism, but modernity has been obsessed with the idea of materialism. Descartes on materialism has affected our culture.

Can government be organized in another way? Can the notions of good and evil, and sin and pride, be incorporated into governmental affairs? Perhaps. I think it really requires an individual, or a group of individuals, to provide the necessary leadership. I am somewhat optimistic about the ability for this to happen because in 1979, I remember a moment where in the depths of despair, I didn't feel as though we could save ourselves. I felt with Afghanistan being invaded, with the hostages still being held in Iran, with an inflation rate of 20%, I really didn't see much hope for this nation. And yet, interestingly, after the 1980 election, maybe I'm attributing too much to Ronald Reagan, maybe this would have happened anyway, nonetheless I felt there was a kind of restoration of faith. Not so much my belief that America would prosper economically, but we were regaining an optimism about the future, a characteristic that I believe is necessary to bring about desirable changes in the culture.

This positive vision was restored by one person, by his leadership. I think that there is a kind of leadership capability that would lead to changes in the way in which we conduct our governmental affairs. It's not all material, as you quite rightly point out, but it is very much related to people coming along saying, 'we're going to reform this system, we're going to change it'. And I think despite the emphasis on materialism, it's possible to do that. I've seen it in my lifetime. I've seen one of the most dramatic political changes of the 20th century and maybe even of the last 200 years -- going from the depths of despair to a sense that there is some hope for America.

WS: I kind of agree with you, Herb, but for a different reason. I would analyze your 1979 experience a little differently. What none of us were aware of in 1979 was the erosion within the Soviet empire. Ronald Reagan came along and upped the ante. He rearmed America dramatically, forcing them to put their chips on the table. When they tried to put more chips on the table, they fell apart. They went bankrupt. There had been tremendous erosion. A huge number of people within the power structure and outside the power structure were in revolt for a whole variety of reasons. Many people could not live with the kinds of people they were meeting, the non-valued, non-spiritualized people that Communism had produced. So there was everything from religious rebellion to the resentment of the insider who travelled to Switzerland and Japan and saw a much higher standard of living. Clearly, the system wasn't working.

Reagan was the man who captured the moment. I think he rearmed because he thought a serious threat was at our door. By rearming, he exposed the hollowness of that threat, and that society.

HL: I think people in New York sense intuitively that there's decay, and that the decay is profound. I don't know if people can understand the degree of malaise that exists in this society in this state. It is very widespread. There isn't a person that I've talked to, and I've travelled to every hamlet in New York, who doesn't say 'I want to get my pension and get the hell out of here. I cannot tolerate living in New York'.

Commentary: ER

William Stern was the campaign finance chairman for Mario Cuomo's successful 1982 gubernatorial race. Governor Cuomo appointed him chairman of the Urban Development Corporation (UDC), a state authority created to build housing and commercial facilities. Because he was already a successful businessman, Mr. Stern welcomed the opportunity for public service.

His tenure was brief, however. As recounted in the following interview, Mr. Stern was forced to spend UDC funds in ways he thought wasteful and unrelated to the authority's central purpose. Political considerations determined the selection of contractors, staff, investment bankers, and projects. In particular, he felt the relative ease with which UDC can issue long-term debt has led to enormous financial abuses.

Indeed, while most New Yorkers are aware of the economic damage done by Albany's tax hikes, the sharp increase in state debt has received scant notice. Since the start of the Cuomo Administration, however, total state and authority debt has risen 106%, far outpacing the 86% rise in state taxes over that period. At the end of fiscal 1992, the total debt load of New York State and its public authorities stood at $62.1 billion. By comparison, state tax collections that year were "only" $28.3 billion.

New York is the nation's debt capital. As the following charts indicate this is a deserved title.

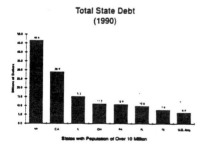

We surpass second ranked California (a state with a much larger population) by $17.7 billion, or 61% according to Census Bureau data for 1990. Whether measured relative to population, personal income, or property valuation, the burden of tax-supported debt in New York State is many times greater than that of the median state:

Tax Supported Debt, 1991

	New York	Median State
Debt per capita	$1,360 (6)	$391
Debt as % Full Property Valuation	5.7% (1)	1.0%
Debt as % Personal Income	6.1% (7)	2.2%

New York state's ranking in parenthesis.

Source: Moody's Investors Service.

The credit rating on New York's tax supported bonds is the worst among the 50 states, according to one rating agency. But tax supported debt, which consists mainly of General Obligation bonds, is not the biggest debt problem facing the state. In fact, G.O. bonds represent less than one-twelfth of all outstanding state debt. Since 1988 voters have rejected every proposed G.O. bond issue, most recently the $800 million infrastructure bond put on the ballot by Mario Cuomo in 1992.

Stymied by the voters, the Governor has turned to state authorities for financing:

Table 1: Total Outstanding State and Authority Debt in NYS

	(in millions)			Percent
	1982	1992	Change	Change
General Obligation	$3,734.1	$5,081.3	$1,347.2	36.1%
Lease-Purchase/Contractual Obligation	4,062.0	16,745.0	12,683.0	312.2
State-Guaranteed Authority	501.0	498.0	(3.0)	-0.6
Authority Debt with Moral Obligation	12,541.0	8,460.0	(4,081.0)	-32.5
Total State Debt	20,838.1	30,784.3	9,946.2	47.7
Other Authority Debt	9,397.1	31,361.2	21,964.1	233.7
Total State and Authority Debt	30,235.2	62,145.5	31,910.3	105.5

New York's 18 largest public authorities--the list includes the Dormitory, Metropolitan Transit, Power, Thruway, and Triborough Bridge and Tunnel Authorities, as well as Urban Development Corporation and the Municipal Assistance Corporation (MAC)--have $100 million or more in debt outstanding; 13 have over $1 billion in outstanding debt. In contrast, ten years ago (1982) there were 15 authorities with $100 million or more debt, and only six with debt in excess of $1 billion.

As shown in Table 1, the fastest growing type of state debt is lease-purchase or contractual obligation debt. Under "lease-back" agreements, state authorities issue bonds to finance specific construction projects, which are in turn "leased" to the state. Each year the legislature appropriates taxpayer funds to pay "rent" to the authority. The rent, of course, is set equal to the debt service on the authority bonds.

A prime example of such agreements involves UDC and state prisons. In 1981 voters rejected a proposed $500 million G.O. bond issue for prison construction--slamming the front door shut on such borrowing. So the Cuomo Administration went around to the back door, and ordered UDC to build them instead.

The largest form of state debt--other authority debt--is not supported by the state, even in the "moral obligation" sense. Although the state is under no legal obligation to help, it is inconceivable that a state authority would be allowed to default. The 1975 fiscal crisis, for example, was precipitated by a UDC note default. Although short-term notes are neither legal nor moral obligations of New York State, Albany provided the necessary funds.

Public authorities were originally intended to be temporary entities, created to build particular projects. Authority debt was supposed to be self-liquidating, serviced by revenues generated by the projects-- dormitories, for example. To our knowledge, no authorities have gone "out of business". In recent years authority borrowing has become a device for forcing voters to pay for projects they do not want, and for financing ordinary budget expenses.

A particularly flagrant abuse occurred when the state "sold" Attica prison to UDC for $200 million in 1990, to plug a budget gap. The UDC sold bonds to pay for the purchase; the state will eventually repurchase the prison at a cost, in interest and principle, more than double the original one-shot benefit.

Not all state officials welcome the gimmicks. In 1991 Comptroller

Edward V. Regan sued to block the sale of $80 million in Thruway Authority "pothole bonds." The bond proceeds were to be transferred to the state Department of Transportation, to finance ordinary road maintenance. In effect, the scheme would have used dedicated toll revenues to help close the budget gap. The real reason for the Authority's toll hikes, according to Mr. Regan, was "to provide additional state operating funds, making the action nothing more than a sophisticated, albeit, presumably legal, money laundering scheme between the State and the Authority."

Shortly after New York's 1975 financial crisis, a state panel said Albany should set up a commission to oversee the authorities. The resulting Public Authority Control Board does a good job of protecting bondholders by evaluating the economic viability of individual projects. But the PACB does nothing for the taxpayers. The larger questions of whether the project is in the public interest, or whether it is better done by an on-budget agency or by the private sector, are "left to the legislature."

While he was Comptroller, Ned Regan proposed amending the state constitution to prohibit the state from supporting debt sold without voter approval. Under his amendment, authority debt would require approval by three-fifths of the Assembly and Senate. The legislature should do this, and simultaneously require that governed authority personnel be governed by the same conflict of interest and competitive contracting rule that regulate--however imperfectly--ordinary state agencies.

Otherwise, the cynicism expressed by William Stern and others about the role of government will continue to be justified.

14 Interview: Thomas Tisch

TT: There are four conditions which are necessary for any urban environment to be successful. First, you have to have the right investment in infrastructure, second, you need a reasonable dialog and accommodation on the issue of race. Third, you have to have a labor management dialog for the city workforce that makes sense. And fourth, you have to have a commitment to creating an additional tax base.

I am always struck at how these forces relate to the building of a great city. For example, in the late 1950s Atlanta and Birmingham were virtually the same size, with apparently identical prospects for future growth. But Atlanta moved ahead because of its investment in infrastructure that made it a transportation hub. And also, because it had a tradition of a black middle class and black institutions in the city. Therefore, rich/poor and class issues were not characterized as racial issues the way they have been in New York.

Boston has a different accommodation on the issue of race. It is a substantially segregated city but there, as well every issue is not framed as a racial issue. I am not saying this is good, I'm just telling it the way it is. In addition, the business community of Boston has hung together cohesively, and they have been able to draw upon the vast educational institutions, which is a form of an investment in infrastructure -- both human and physical. To see the difference between Boston and New York, just take a look at Boston's leadership in Bio-technology and medical firms. Boston-based institutions get a disproportionate share of medical research grants and the President's Science Awards that are given out each year. Many New York institutions have seen their medical research decimated over the past fast few years, and are now fancy primary-care facilities. In terms of national research, and peer review, the action in bio-medical research is not in New York. The same thing is true in the computer sciences.

Yes, we have a lot of financial technology, but I'm afraid it is much more cyclical in nature.

HL: Very good point!

ER: Is it because we don't have a Harvard here to attract people? The city government isn't interested in financing the sort of industrial parks that have been successful in Boston.

TT: Well, I don't believe it's a question of financing, but rather of three or four viruses which we have here in New York. First of all, the cost of doing business in this town is very, very high relative to the cost of doing business anywhere else. And the myth, that you have to be in New York to be successful has been shattered in a great number of industries. CNN shows that you can run a network very successfully in Atlanta. Wal-mart and JC Penney show that you can run a retailing operation outside of New York. It used to be that you had to be here, but that is an illusion today.

Taxes, at both the city and state level, are an enormous vice that pushes businesses out of New York. Years ago, Andy Tobias did a terrific piece on New York's Unincorporated Business Tax and how it drove him to leave New York. The fact is that big businesses cut a side deal with the city and state to keep the cost of doing business in New York reasonably tolerable, but, those deals come with two enormous costs: first, businesses which make the deal tend to keep quiet about the problems of doing business in New York and, therefore, we lose our honest civic-minded business community. And second, who speaks for the middle class and small businessman?

HL: Well, this comes back to the issue you raised before, Tom. If, in fact, the way to get a special deal is to threaten to leave NY, and if NBC decides to leave for New Jersey and gets a special deal, then I think the system is ultimately compromised. Large firms get preferential treatment because they have a voice, not because they are better for the economy.

TT: And in NY, when NBC gets a special deal, it gets a $10 million advantage to it's nearly identical rival, CBS. So what is the guy at CBS supposed to do now? If CBS has a stock market multiple of 15 or so, then the special tax deal represents 3 or 4 percent of its enterprise value. Just the tax deal alone. At a certain point a guy says to himself, you want me to be nice, but I get nothing from being nice. The only way I get the most competitive cost of doing business in New York is if I threaten to leave. But one has to be both big and politically connected and willing to threaten to leave to play the game. The middle class and small businessman can't play. They have no voice.

The question remains who speaks for the middle class? In the 1980s, the Fortune 500 companies laid off 2 million people. Maybe the whole economy created 18 million jobs, so the jobs came from someplace else. So all we do is make the environment in the city the worst possible environment for business. You advertise this fact when big business gets a special deal in order to stay here. We should instead be doing the fundamental and structural things to reform the cost and burdens of doing business for everyone, so that we do not cannibalize our existing tax base and prevent newcomers from coming here.

The structural imbalance of New York doesn't just relate to the business community, it is also apparent in the housing situation. People talk about the homeless problem. I define the homeless problem more broadly than most; it is the inability of the private sector and private resources to house an astounding percentage of the city's population. Each night, the public sector is responsible for housing 950,000 people in a city of 7 million. That's right, 950,000 people a night living in *in rem* housing and city projects. It's amazing when you think of the city as an organism, that anybody can exist in it. Its as if the city were a heart riddled with arterial sclerosis. And most amazingly, there is very little public discussion of the depths of New York's housing crisis. You can't find that housing number in the *New York Times*. When I recently read a story about Laura Blackburn's couch, buried somewhere in the story was that 950,000 people flow through the city housing departments.

HL: Well, Bill Tucker uses that number as well.

TT: They're extraordinary numbers, and nobody talks about it. Perhaps Mayor Dinkins is a mathematical genius because he has figured out that enough people depend on city housing to virtually ensure his re-election.

ER: You mentioned bio-technology and the fact that the city hasn't developed that. But Boston, of course, has the 'Route 128 effect'...

TT: And Harvard and other institutions.

ER: But we have Columbia. In the right environment, Columbia could be for NYC what Harvard is to Boston.

TT: Not in the sciences.

ER: Columbia Presbyterian Medical Center?

TT: Not really. New York's position in the sciences has weakened substantially over the last two decades as other regions have invested tremendously.

ER: But we have the intellectual and scientific infrastructure here that I would put up against anybody. But it seems to me that the bio-technology companies like campus settings. We may be at a geographical disadvantage because we cannot provide those settings. I think there are some disadvantages that we have that are just irreducible, that we're stuck with, being New York. There are certain infrastructures that we simply cannot provide.

TT: Maybe.

HL: The city's disadvantages are mainly of its own making, however. How else can you explain why almost all of the major pharmaceutical companies are on the other side of the Hudson. Here, you have to look not only at the opportunities for expansion, but at the tax base, and the advantages they get for being in New Jersey. I mean Warner-Lambert, Johnson & Johnson, they're all there. Let's come back to the four points you raised before, which are interesting; apply them to New York State. Let's say you were in a position to wave a magic wand and you were to talk about the race question, the tax question, the infrastructure question and labor management.

TT: I'm not the only person talking about these issues. The Manhattan Institute's *City Journal* has been addressing them brilliantly for years.

Clearly, we have to find ways of reducing the tax burden and other costs of living in New York to make the city and state more competitive with other jurisdictions. We have also become tremendously parochial in our outlook and we should look to the immensely creative things that are going on in other jurisdictions.

In labor management, the city should consider doing what the airlines did after deregulation, which is to go to a two tier system of A and B employees. You 'grandfather' certain employees -- the A's who will continue to receive existing wages and benefits -- and the new employees -- the B's, come in at prevailing market rates. Additionally, any Mayor should be prepared to take some very tough strikes in this town, and be prepared to break the monopoly of the municipal unions. Philadelphia, for example, has gone through the crisis. The fact is you've got to be prepared to lose an election on that issue alone. Unless we solve the labor issue, the city is doomed.

On the question of race, we have to neutralize it as an issue, to move beyond it and define all issues in terms of the shared interests of all New Yorkers. Tragically, the issue of race is often used for short-term political gain. I often think of Mayor Dinkins as a black-zionist who cares passionately about people with the same skin color, but the Mayor has to be the Mayor of all the people. In a way the race issue is on the table because, as Henry Kissinger said about academia, the fighting is so vicious because the stakes are so small. Economically, if there is no economic opportunity and no job growth it is easy to politicize people to fight for rights as group rights. Therefore, people should not be afraid to make the economic growth arguments before all audiences.

It is interesting that when Dick Ravitch ran for mayor, he found it virtually impossible to speak before a black church. Quietly, in the last weeks of the campaign, he got into a black church, I think in East New York. He said it was one of the most extraordinary, incandescent moments of his election, because he spoke about why he was against commercial rent control. He said he was against commercial rent control for the following reasons: number one, it entrenches the least efficient operator, who is going to charge you more money and if somebody more efficient wants to come in, they have no opportunity to do so. If Wal-mart wanted to deliver cheaper prices and wanted to rent a store, they'd be precluded from the market. And number two, he said that everybody wants a lot of programs, but if you want programs, you have to have the tax base support them. And without the property tax base, how are we going to get those programs? And he said that the people there responded very, very positively to him. He was able to show how free-market economics can make a difference in everybody's lives.

I don't agree with Jack Kemp on all issues, but he's right on the issue of economic empowerment, and yet many people -- liberals in particular, are afraid to accept them for what they are -- a necessary way out of our current urban problems. Without economic growth, the city will remain mired in its existing problems and racial dialogue. And if one truly believes in economic growth, one has to be willing to take on the most absurd of our policies in this city and state, namely rent control. I think the most interesting way to run for mayor in this town is to emphasize private sector growth, and use rent control as your metaphor. We should back a candidate who's willing to take this one on. In fact, since the co-oping movement is so great in Manhattan and since the homeowners are the backbone of Brooklyn, Queens and Staten Island, I think you could get their support and win if you frame the issue the right way.

So my theory is, in a way, that the time is getting riper to make private sector job growth the number one goal and use rent control as the metaphor for a whole set of economic burdens which have impeded growth in New York. To me there's only one way to run for mayor this year, and that's to make private sector jobs your number one goal, and just run it on TV. You will want to cite Steve Kagann's statistics that show private sector jobs have declined over the last 30 years because of high taxes on NYC businesses. If you want business as usual, elect the usual politicians.

ER: Of course, Steve shows that the rise in public employment has offset some of the decline in private jobs. The subtext there is that the upward line of government employees is filled with minorities.

TT: So, in the end, what good will it do for anyone if the city's economy will consist entirely of government workers. Who will pay the taxes? The fact is that in the next 36 months there's either going to be a profound change at City Hall, or there's going to be a major fiscal crisis.

I used to own a lot of NY State Municipal bonds; I don't want to own any today. Although you receive 100 basis point advantage versus Treasuries, when the crisis hits, you could have significant principal risk because municipal bonds are held significantly by municipal bond funds. There is a chance that when the people who go to cocktail parties say they bought municipals this week, suddenly go to the cocktail party and say they pulled out, the funds will be forced to sell the good bonds because there'll be no market for the bad bonds. Additionally, there has been a lack of honesty in state government about fiscal matters that allow the state to say it has a balanced budget. The fact is that without any employment growth, we've doubled the taxpayer-supported debt in the last 5 years, from $12 billion to $24 billion. So, one way or another, the structural deficit is there. The "one-shots" in the state budget have been enormous -- the raiding of the insurance fund and the sale of Attica and the Thruway for example. It all adds up. And the accumulation of it, when it unwinds, is going to force people to reshape government, but without any of the honest debate that's really needed to do it right.

HL: Tom, let me back up. I think you've raised the issue very effectively. I certainly couldn't do it any better. But let's assume we do not have this crisis, because the crisis, quite obviously, would be the catalyst for some kind of reform. Is there another way?

TT: There is a way short of a crisis, but it will take a lot of honesty and political resolve to get there. Massachusetts, for example, has had substantial reform without a crisis. Fortunately for Massachusetts, the voters there elected a principled, honest, and tough Governor who is willing to lay out the agenda honestly in a campaign and follow it out in office. In New York our problems are much more entrenched at both the city and state levels which are umbilically tied. We also have more diffused government because of the role that authorities play in the state.

Historically, the last time the state was in the crisis it is today was in the 1840s when after the success of the Erie Canal the state financed many ill-advised capital projects with debt. The state was forced to go, hat in hand, to the federal government looking for a bail out. As a result of that experience, the voters of New York enacted a balanced budget amendment which required any state-funded debt to be approved by the voters. Over the last twenty years we have honored that amendment more in its breach than in its observance. I'm hopeful that we can resolve our problems without a crisis, but history shows that it is usually a crisis which brings together the forces of change.

And we must remember that any change will probably have to be made in the context of revenue declines at both the state and city level. The state and city have both benefited from the enormous run up in stock and bond prices, close to 15% per year, over the last decade which have filled governments coffers with tremendous capital gains receipts. These are clearly unsustainable. Additionally, the city will have to deal with the weak real estate market and declining property tax receipts due to historical over-assessments.

ER: You mentioned that certiory proceedings haven't really hit yet. So when they do, assessments will plummet.

TT: The average office building in New York City is probably 25% over-assessed. For example, take an average twenty or thirty year old Class A office building. City taxes are probably $11 a foot; operating costs are $8 a foot, so it costs $19 a foot in cash to open your doors for a tenant. In addition, you have to give the tenant a $60 work letter, and also a year's free rent. So even without a mortgage on the building, the best you can hope to do in midtown is break even with rents in the upper $20s. And all of this assumes that the building has no mortgage. Downtown, things are worse.

The fact is that property assessments are based on four things: replacement costs, rental income, cost of comparable structures and construction costs. The city doesn't want to face the fact that the market is materially hurt and may not be coming back. For a building owner, you don't know if you're better off having your building vacant and getting your taxes down, or renting the building and losing money. It's a very tough equation, nobody wants to face the reality.

ER: The Japanese, on the other hand, don't care whether they're losing money now. To them there are only three things in real estate: location, location and location. If they're where they want to be, vis-a-vis the rest of the city, they know that values will come back.

TT: Anybody who thinks that might be kidding themselves. Buildings in NYC, free and clear and untenanted, are worth virtually nothing today. Will they come back? Yes, when we have enough employment growth to begin to fill them. The city doesn't care, in the end, who owns the buildings. They don't care that Mr. X sells it to the next guy as long as they keep getting their piece of the action through taxes.

But the cash cost of the real estate taxes and regulatory burdens is too high, and ultimately, without correction, there's going to be a surge of abandonments. Once the price gets driven down to zero, people may begin to abandon them.

HL: You said a moment ago, Tom, that the political race in NY, should be run with some understanding of the integrity of the private sector, and some reformulation of the way in which you do business in the private sector. Suppose you were running a campaign. Recognizing the array of political forces you would have to address, how would you organize a campaign, absent the crisis that you talked about, and given the unwillingness of a good many people in the business community to even recognize that a crisis exists?

TT: As I said before, I think the only thing you can do is talk about the problems honestly. My sense is that in the governor's race, and in the mayor's race, the best you can do is tell it honestly, and if it doesn't hit now, if you lay it out the right way, without getting vituperative about it, then one of these days you're going to come back and collect on your willingness to be candid. I think the tragedy of NY is that Lew Lehrman laid out the right agenda, but he just didn't stay around to collect on it. Governor Cuomo, on the other hand, has been more Machiavellian, to say it nicely, and as a consequence the political debate in the state has been destroyed more than anybody could have imagined. And more destructive, is what has happened to the idea of governance, to the idea of personal responsibility in the political dialogue. Therefore, it's going to be harder to recreate than people might think. But I think there is, for the first time, beginning to be some understanding of the depths of the issues, a kind of resonance. While I believe the *New York Times* is lost on many economic issues, it's waking up to the issues close to home and giving much better coverage to both Albany and City Hall. An example is Kevin Sack's recent piece in the Sunday Magazine on political entrenchment in Albany.

ER: But the question is, can a candidate win on these issues?

TT: The question is not whether you can win or not win on the issue. It is what do you do about it when you get there. Because the things that have to be done are so painful and so bleak, you may have the people's support, but still not succeed in changing things because you're not going to have the institutional support of the government itself.

HL: You laid it out, I think, very well. Ed Rendel did what was necessary in Philadelphia. He faced down the union, the Sanitation Union. He took a terrible blow in the *Philadelphia Enquirer*, and he came up on top. I think you may have to do that. I think you have to at some point suggest that we cannot tolerate the 271,000 state employees, with a $59.9 billion budget in this state. We're driving private capital out of existence, you've made that point. I think we've simply got to say that there's a better way of doing business. The blueprint for it, notwithstanding the obvious differences, are found in Massachusetts. That's the blueprint.

TT: Exactly. With all the pain, and the pain will be greater in NY.

HL: Oh absolutely.

ER: But is Governor Weld of Massachusetts going to be re-elected?

HL: He will unquestionably be re-elected. But I think Tom's point is somewhat different. Tom is really suggesting what you do when you get there. I think one of the things that you do when you get there, assuming that it's someone with genuine integrity who wants to make the change, is to say I just can't worry about a second term. Because once you start doing that, once you say how do I put a constituency together, particularly as a Republican, it becomes impossible to make the reforms that are needed.

TT: And you can bring very, very good people into governance of the state. Governor Cuomo hasn't made Albany an exciting place for good people. It doesn't mean that it can't be done.

HL: I think, more and more, there's a growing understanding. The consciousness in this state has changed. There are fundamental differences. I was up in Buffalo several weeks ago, I mentioned this to Ed, I was at a rally and a number of the people who came own trucking firms. We've been losing trucking firms to the tune of about 100 a year in NYS. We're down to about 220 left. Most of them have simply moved across the border into Pennsylvania, where it's a lot cheaper to do business. And these guys are fed up, but the people who came to the demonstration were primarily truckers themselves, who are losing jobs. They don't want to move to Pennsylvania. They are eager to remain in the state, and they are out there demonstrating with their employers. The very impressive dimension of this activity was that many of these truckers are black, and they came to my rally. There was a fellow from the NBC station in Buffalo, who said to one of the truckers: why are you here for this conservative Republican, Herb London. He said: Herb London wants to create jobs, the democrats are destroying jobs. Now for a rather unsophisticated trucker to make this remark and to say 'I'm here with my employer, because I want to see jobs remain in this state,' I think is a very significant breakthrough. That's not the kind of guy you would expect to see at a demonstration with a conservative Republican. So, I think there is a change.

TT: In the same way, Andrew Sullivan, editor of the *New Republic*, said at the time of the Republican Convention that Pat Buchanan is not a conservative, he's counter-cultural.

HL: I wrote the same thing myself in the *NY Post*. I wrote an editorial where I said precisely the same.

TT: I didn't see your piece, but Andrew Sullivan stated it very clearly--a true conservative is for fiscal responsibility, individual freedom, and political moderation--and that sounds alright to me.

Commentary: HL

As Tom Tisch, a noted business leader in New York, argues, a city is a corporate entity with its own unique social compact. When that compact isn't insured, when the groups aren't involved in a symbiotic relationship, when a Hobbesian world view of each against all prevails, cities are in jeopardy. New York is certainly one of those cities. The bonds of social harmony are being stretched to the limit. As a result, the creative impulses in the city are seeking other outlets.

New York is no longer the business capital of the world. The illusion that a business must be in the city has been shattered. New

York may cling to its mythology of the world's business capital, but the reality of urban life suggests a dispersal of assets. As Tom Tisch illustrates, New York has become the center of political deals in which the idiom of urban life is who is getting what from whom at the best price.

Because the city takes care of so many people in so many ways, politics is largely a question of servicing populations perceived to be in greatest need. Close to 1 million people live in public housing; 1.1 million are on welfare; more than a million people live in rent controlled and rent stabilized housing. Is it any wonder most politicians who are opposed to the expansion of government authority lose elections?

In addition, as Mr. Tisch notes, municipal unions dominate city affairs. Compounding this labor problem is a race problem, since a disproportionate share of the more than 250,000 city employees are Black. Retrenchment, therefore, invariably takes the form of black-white animosity. But if that retrenchment doesn't occur, opportunities for those in the private sector are restricted. A decline in private sector employment is directly related to the expansion of government jobs and the attendant increase in taxes.

As in the case with almost everyone interviewed for this book, Tom Tisch doesn't envision any facile solutions to what ails the city and state. Absent a crisis, one can expect business as usual. In fact, despite a proportional decline in private sector jobs, the state has doubled the taxpayer supported debt in the last 5 years from $12 to $24 billion. The city is over a billion dollars out of balance and the state somewhere between 3 and 4 billion dollars in arrears annually.

With the economy restrained by *dirigiste* concerns, real estate has been dramatically overassessed. The reasons are clear: city taxes are greater than operating costs. The best any property owner can expect is to break even, with the hope somewhere over the horizon that his building will appreciate in value and a buyer appears at his doorstep. At the moment, as Tom Tisch appropriately notes, a building owner doesn't know if he is better off having his building vacant and thereby having his taxes reduced, or renting his space at reduced rates and losing capital. With tax and regulation burdens overwhelming, most commercial property owners can't possibly see a pot of gold at the end of the rainbow. What they do see is a surge of abandonment with disastrous consequences for city finances.

Unless government officials help to shape a resurgence in the private sector so that tenants want to rent commercial space and jobs are created, New York will sink inextricably into the depths of despair. It is clear that government directed policies don't assist the private sector, notwithstanding so many of the exaggerated claims attached to MITI in Japan. More than anything else, the private sector seems to thrive on a government that gets out of the way, that doesn't place impediments in the way of private enterprise, such as gratuitous regulations or extortionate taxes.

Not only are the visible taxes and regulations impediments to development, but there are also hidden taxes, such as the utility tax, the petroleum tax and the hospital tax. These are taxes that are unseen, decided on without the peoples' consent, and predicated on the view that what we can't pay for now we will impose a tax on a generation in the future. If taxation without representation was the calling card for revolution in our past, it is obviously a rallying cry against policies in the present as well.

Conclusion

Taxes. Rent control. Welfare reform. Government regulations. Political gridlock. The topics covered in these interviews converge at one overarching point: the economic future. At the start of 1994, New Yorkers still feel the pain of recession. We feel tentative about our economic prospects, and for good reason. Since the official end of the recession in 1991, the number of jobs nationwide has grown by about 2 million. But in that same period, New York State has continued to lose jobs--about 272,000.

While the rest of the region is recovering slowly, New York remains mired in one of the worst recessions of the past 20 years.

Entrepreneurs will think twice before locating in a state where personal income taxes take 7.875% of every additional dollar of earnings. Many large corporations have already left. Thanks to Mr. Cuomo's 15% surcharge, the state's top corporate tax rate-10.35%-exceeds that of every state except Connecticut and Pennsylvania. And there are the fees, the fines, and the special charges that the state slaps on everything from truckers to hospitals to local governments. Revenues from these hidden taxes total about $4.7 billion. That figure has doubled in just the past five years.

State officials insist, however, that high taxes and interventionist policies are not responsible for the dismal economic performance. The Clinton Administration pushes this perverse philosophy further, claiming that its tax hikes and proposed health care mandates will actually create jobs and economic growth.

But studies show otherwise. Back in 1990, the *Wall Street Journal* compared rates of job creation in low and high tax states. [1] According to the study, the ten lowest taxed states enjoyed average job growth of

---

[1] David Littman, "High-Tax States Are Low-Growth States," Wall Street Journal, August 6, 1990. (Op-ed page.)

77% over the preceding 15 years, versus only 18% average growth in the ten highest taxed states. And wouldn't you know it, when states were ranked by "tax effort", or tax collections as a percent of the state's underlying wealth, New York emerged as the **most heavily taxed state in the nation.**

New York's unenviable "number one" ranking has solidified since then. In fact, from 1989 through 1993 Albany increased taxes by over $1 billion annually. As one might expect, the employment picture worsened. New York lost jobs at an average annual rate of 1.13% over the 1989-1992 period, versus a 0.58% annual gain for the nation over the same period.

New York has lost more than 571,000 jobs since the onset of recession in July 1990. Restoring the loss will be difficult, in part because people are moving out:

MOVING OUT: STATES WITH THE LARGEST OUT-MIGRATIONS (1985-1990)

State	Moved Out	Moved In	Net Gain/(Loss)
New York	1,548,507	1,341,345	(207,162)
Texas	1,495,475	1,532,107	36,722
Florida	1,059,931	2,672,194	1,461,550
Illinois	1,009,922	870,562	(162,285)
California	801,267	3,473,441	2,672,194
Pennsylvania	771,709	792,595	20,886
Ohio	763,625	691,552	(72,073)
New Jersey	763,123	781,007	17,884
Virginia	635,695	1,012,291	376,596
Michigan	606,472	547,780	(58,692)

Source: U.S. Bureau of the Census.

During the last half the 1980s, 1.34 million people moved into New York State. Half of them were foreign immigrants. But over the same period almost 1.55 million people left the state - the greatest out-flow of any state. Overall, the state lost over 200,000 people to out-migration. Only Louisiana, a state dependent on a declining oil industry, lost more.

During the 1980s, New York State's population increased by 2.5%, or at about one-quarter the nation's 9.8% rate. The subdued growth makes New York a less attractive location for consumer services and retailing operations.

More importantly, the employability of the state's population has deteriorated:

- The proportion of the non-English speaking population is growing. In three of the five boroughs of New York City it exceeds 10%.

- The white population of New York State has shrunk dramatically since 1970, mainly because of shifts out of New York City. The incoming minorities are ill trained for jobs that depend on abstract reasoning or information processing. Until the New York City school system undergoes a complete transformation, inner city employment prospects will remain grim.

- A growing share of the New York State population is 65 and older. The median age of state residents is higher than for the U.S. as a whole.

In his 1994 State of the State message, Governor Cuomo said "Jobs should come first, not welfare." Rhetoric aside, his plan does little to create jobs or control welfare. The tax cuts are laughingly small. Indeed, the centerpiece - a reduction in the corporate income tax surcharge - merely reduces a tax that the state was scheduled to eliminate last year, but couldn't because of a looming budget gap.

Mr. Cuomo's plan relies on government spending to create jobs. Last year's list of "economic development" projects included swimming pools and gymnasiums, a $50,000 grant to explore building a sports arena in Nassau County, and $500,000 for "assessing and improving the competitiveness of forest industry firms of fewer than 200 employees." The Governor will make an additional $32 billion available for infrastructure this year. President Clinton, he boasts, wasn't able to get half that sum for the entire nation.

It is entirely possible that a strong economic recovery in neighboring states, where taxes are less burdensome, will stimulate a modest rebound here. Income gains in selected industries are already pushing state revenues up faster than inflation. The budget crisis will not end so quickly, however. Future generations will have to pay for the budget gimmicks used to make ends meet during the Cuomo years.

Years of issuing debt to cover current expenses have depressed New York's credit rating to second lowest of the 50 states. Some of the more egregious one-shot budget gimmicks such as the "sale" of Attica prison to a state authority, have been challenged in state courts. The Governor's call for a constitutional amendment limiting debt issuance comes far too late in the day.

In 1992 Americans protested that their government wasn't working, and voted for change. The word doesn't seem to have reached Albany.

Epilogue

When Mark Twain read his own obituary and noted that claims of his death had been greatly exaggerated, it was a mildly amusing tale. In New York, however, predictions of the death of this once great state should be taken quite seriously.

New York has 7.2% of the nation's population and 15% of the states' accumulated debt. It has lost 40% of all the jobs that have disappeared since the recession technically began in June 1989.

In New York people have been voting with their feet. The vast majority of people who are leaving the state are taxpayers with financial options. The poor, the indigent, the welfare recipients do not generally leave the state.

So far in the '90s, New York has lost about 500,000 residents. The signs are clear: Those older than 60 can't wait to get their pensions and leave for greener pastures--places without state personal income tax, such as Florida. Those about 30 want to leave and establish a business in a state without a corporate income tax, such as Texas or Nevada.

New York's 7.7875% income tax is 54% above the average of the four contiguous states. Since Mario Cuomo became governor in 1983, the tax rate has gone down, but actual taxes per individual have gone up, dramatically. In part this is due to state mandates that force localities to bear the brunt of state decisions without the consequent flow of tax dollars. As the January 1994 issue of *Money* magazine pointed out, the New York State tax bill for a typical family of four is almost 7 times as high as Alaska's tab and the highest rate in the nation by far.

Localities have only two options in response to State mandates: raise property taxes or raise sales taxes. New York, with $3,267 per capita, has the second highest State and local taxes in the nation, 62% higher than the national average. On $1,000 of personal income, state and local taxes in New York were at $155.35 in 1990, or the second highest rate in the nation. The state's 10.35% corporate tax is the second highest in the nation, after Connecticut, and 53% above the national average. From 1988 to the present, the corporate net income tax burden as a percentage of the national average has been highest in New York State, 98% higher than the national average.

The state discourages business enterprise by taxing capital gains at a 36.5% rate. In New York City, capital gains are taxed at an astonishing 39.75% rate, the highest in the nation.

The numbers suggest why private capital is being crowded out of existence here. The statistics also indicate why New York lags dramatically behind the rest of the nation in jobs production.

During the 1980s New York ranked 47th of the 50 states in job creation. If New York had been closer to the national average in job creation, during the '80s, the government could have paid the bills despite the Cuomo Administration's avaricious appetite for spending. What has actually occurred is a dramatic increase in the state workforce and a decline in private sector jobs. Here are the facts: The state payroll expanded by nearly 1,000 full-time equivalent positions between June 1992 and June 1993, according to the comptroller's statistics. Private sector employment in 1993 totaled 6.34 million, down 41,000 from the previous year. Since 1990 the state workforce has been reduced by 17,414, mostly through attrition, but even after this reduction is calculated, the state has had an increase of 15,256 jobs, or a 7.43% jump since Cuomo took office in 1983.

To meet its legal obligation for a balanced budget, the state has gone deeply into debt. New York's per capita debt of $2,869 surpasses the national average by 109%.

Yes, New York is in dire straits, a product of corpulent debt, an addiction to spending, an unprecedented tax burden, and a government that has lost sight of the taxpayers.

It is clear from our analysis and from the interviews with Democrats and Republicans, so-called liberals and conservatives, that there is a desperate need for reform in New York State. If this book has any value, it is in bringing this need to the public's attention so that a genuine debate of the issues can take place.

About the Authors

Herbert London: John M. Olin Professor of Humanities, New York University; candidate for Governor of New York, 1994.

Edwin S. Rubenstein: economic consultant and journalist.

About the Contributors

Herman Badillo: Lawyer, former Deputy Mayor of New York City.

Edward N. Costikyan: Lawyer and former Chairman of the New York Democratic Party.

John J. Gilbert: Former Director of the Rent Stabilization Association.

Joseph R. Holland: New York State Senator.

Stephen Kagann: Former adviser to Mayor Rudolph Giuliani.

Edward I. Koch: Former Mayor of New York City.

Dick Netzer: Professor of Public Administration at New York University.

Clarence D. Rappleyea: Minority leader, New York State Assembly.

Edward V. Regan: Recipient of the Jerome Levy chair at Bard College, former New York State Comptroller.

Edward Reinfurt: Assistant Director of the New York State Business Council.

E.S. Savas: Professor of Management, City University of New York.

Henry J. Stern: Former Executive Director of the Citizens Union, presently New York City Parks Commissioner.
William J. Stern: Businessman and former director of the New York State Urban Development Corporation.

190

Thomas J. Tisch: Managing partner of FLF Associates, a division of Loews Corporation.